In the
Company of
Birds

LINDA JOHNS

NIMBUS
PUBLISHING

The Power and the Glory,
acrylic on canvas, in the parish church,
Louisdale, Cape Breton, Nova Scotia.

For my patient elders, the birds…

Nimbus Publishing Limited
P.O. Box 9301, Station A
Halifax, N.S. B3K 5N5
(902) 455-4286

Design: GDA, Halifax
Printing and binding: Everbest Printing Co. Ltd., Hong Kong

Canadian Cataloguing in Publication Data
Johns, Linda..
In the company of birds
ISBN 1-55109-127-5

1. Wild birds as pets. I. Title.
SF462.5.J64 1995   C818'.5403   C95-950113-4

Introduction

WITHIN THESE PAGES I have blushingly recalled numerous experiences of hilarity, embarrassment, insight and affection whereby many remarkable birds have enriched my life. Even more daringly, I've tried to describe and interpret a little of the artwork connected directly with individual personalities—from a duck with unquenchable joie de vivre, to the ascending spirit of a dying gull; from a snoring rooster slumbering in my lap, to aesthetically-placed starling droppings on an unfinished canvas that were incorporated into the finished work.

When I wrote *Sharing a Robin's Life* (Nimbus 1993), I included a few reflections that had resulted in art but omitted any specific mention of my lifework. That story was 'County's,' but in excluding the artwork, only part of the truth was told. In our five-and-a-half-years together, County became the wellspring of my art and taught me to interpret symbolically not only my special relationship with her but also my experiences with other birds.

Through my relationship with County, my thoughts and perceptions flourished and broadened in surprising ways (as many a perplexed curator will confirm). With her constant companionship and inspiration, works involving concepts of light and darkness, growth and decay, unity and dissolution flowed unceasingly. After her physical loss, images of transcendence and the indestructibility of the spirit gained greater significance.

When interacting with symbolic forms from traditional cultures, County glowed with the inspiring renewal of lost wisdom and dignity. Often, she was expressed unfolding a new radiant energy like the new energy she released in me and my artwork. Her form, as she moved from one threshold into another—nestling, adult, mother—mirrored the eternal spirit in constant flow. Brooding her eggs signified for me the concentrated energy within the stillness of the centre that results in new growth, in transformation. Her protective devotion to her babes also drew me to focus on the constant nurturing necessary for inner growth. Even her nestlings came to signify a new threshold of consciousness, a need for spiritual nourishment, a fresh start. Thus, from an actual downy nestling gaping for food came the suggestion of the hunger for fulfilment felt at each level in our inner development.

County's essence still guides my continual probing of the spirit's journey and reinforces my trust that all beings share in the pull towards the light, not just the human ones.

As I emerged one night from the university library, two-and-one-half years after County's departure into another reality, I glanced up at the stars, thoughts of her for once not consciously in my mind. At that moment, visible only to my inner eyes, a tiny glowing ball swept down and hovered over my head momentarily, as though landing, and then swept around before me and flew into my heart. At once, my thoughts overflowed with County. My feelings became incredibly charged.

I treasure the connection she made with me that night, and when my time comes to cross the great threshold, I feel confident that she will be my psychopomp all the way.

Such intimate experiences with one bird inevitably broadened my ruminations on others. Hence, these pages faithfully record not only entertaining interactions with a variety of birds, but also transpersonal reflections as rendered in specific artworks.

It is my hope that these marvellous feathered teachers will challenge the reader's preconceptions as they have mine.

The Secret Spinner,
linoprint.

Prologue

Week after week, within the snug semi-darkness of a hay-filled barn, a hen brooded on her nest. Day after day, she warmed her eggs, turning them periodically and hearing the new heartbeats quicken beneath her. Every morning and evening, for exercise, she was let out of the strong cage protecting her potential family, while chores were done elsewhere; then she was latched safely inside again: predators were never far away.

Early one August morning, after being let out as usual, she couldn't be found when the time came to shut her in. Her owner hunted everywhere in a fever of distraction; he was due to leave immediately for the airport and time was pressing. Then he heard peeping from the cage ... he peered in. One of the eggs was hatching.

CHAPTER ONE

Bubble and Squeak

THAT SAME AUGUST MORNING, several miles away, I was cleaning the pigeons' shelves in the studio. 'Desmond' and 'Molly,' two beautiful chestnut and white Fancy Pigeons with white feathered feet, strutted and cooed mock warnings as they defended their roosts against my invasive ministrations (and occasional tail-tweakings). Suddenly the telephone rang and 'game' was called while I left the room to answer. Moments later I was speeding down the road in the van, turning over in my mind various ways of temporarily housing one newborn chick and a clutch of four-teen eggs on the verge of hatching.

By the time I arrived at the farm, the new chick had been carefully lifted out of his eggshell remnants and transferred to my friend's jacket where he was already soft and dry. Quickly we plugged in the red brooder lamp I had brought and warmed the eggs before wrapping them in sweaters and laying them in a box in the van. Then I climbed into the driver's seat with the chick tucked in warmly against my neck. We were off.

Sadly, the mother hen was never found.

Most of that day I spent in the dining room squinting at a thermometer beside the eggs and adjusting the lamp, trying to maintain a steady heat. A large cardboard box enclosing the nest helped retain the warmth and discourage draughts. The new chick, golden fluff with large dark eyes and a miniature comb, basked in the rosy glow and teetered about on two spindly legs that terminated in a splay of unbelievably tiny toes. He showed little interest in food and I knew he wouldn't need nourishment during the first twenty-four hours after hatching. I cradled him often in my hands too, murmuring into his downy warmth and trying to supply the motherly contact he had been denied so mysteriously. Magically, every now and then, one of the eggs would peep several times and both the chick and I would answer.

About nine o'clock that evening, I heard a scratching sound

in the nest and watched in mounting excitement as one of the eggs wiggled slightly. After a pause, the scratching began again and a tiny hole appeared in the shell. As the hole widened and a crack edged outward, I could see the tip of the new chick's beak as he thrust his head against the shell and the sharp eggtooth cut through the crust. After each pause for rest, he'd cheep from the darkness of his egg and the first chick and I would respond encouragingly; heartened, he'd struggle on again and again. My fingers twitched anxiously to help but I firmly resisted the temptation.

As the crack widened, I could see the inner membrane pulsating with every breath whenever the chick rested; truly, another dimension of existence was revealed within the egg, just as the universe of time and space is cradled within the cosmic egg of creation. After nearly an hour's labour, a mere half-inch of uncut shell separated his inner world from ours, and he strained mightily to cross the threshold. With each thrust, the gap was weakened until finally the shell snapped and parted. In a final effort, he extricated his head and sprawled on the towel, damp and exhausted. Gradually his dark stringiness dried to pearl gray softness but, in spite of my good intentions, I fear I failed to replicate a welcoming motherly hen. As soon as possible he tried, unsuccessfully, to climb back into his shell!

As the days slipped by, the two chicks flourished, but no others hatched and eventually the eggs were removed. I sprinkled a mixture of oatmeal and cornmeal on a small plastic lid and found that tapping my finger on it approximated the sound of hens pecking grain. This stimulated the chicks to eat. Water became intriguing when I dabbled a finger in it, rippling the surface invitingly, or when I set a drop on their beaks to trickle into their mouths. As they began to associate the brightness of light on water with thirst satisfied, they'd touch their beaks to my bright silver ring, lift their heads and swallow expectantly. Their ensuing perplexity was touchingly humorous.

Soon I began releasing an assortment of bugs into their box

and the chicks scrambled about with wild enthusiasm catching them. Centipedes and spiders quickly became favourites. Whenever one of these was grabbed, the lucky chick would scamper about peeping excitedly with the bug clutched firmly in his beak, greatly alarmed lest the other chick steal it. Invariably his exuberant squeaks would attract the other's attention to his prize and the chase was on.

I fell into the habit of calling the chicks 'Bubble and Squeak,' a British idiom for vitality (as well as a culinary dish—*not* chicken) and it was amusing to watch how naturally their developing personalities fitted their names. Bubble the firstborn, golden as the sun, possessed a wonderful gift of inner stillness, being truly an imperturbable bubble in spite of the conflicting currents of his ever-vacillating world. Little gray Squeak, on the other hand, was born with a double helping of inherent anxiety—as evident in his compelling desire to forego the world and return to the egg. Throughout his adolescent months he wore an habitually worried expression, was easily alarmed and trembled all over when nervous or happy. By nature a communicator, he 'squeaked' incessantly in direct contrast to Bubble's calm reticence.

For several weeks I'd also been caring for an incapacitated grackle isolated in a separate room. He had struck a window with shattering force and was fast losing the little locomotive control he had retained. His strength was dwindling steadily and by the time Bubble and Squeak were two weeks old, the grackle was dying and giving off a strange odour. Alarmed lest the chicks contract some mysterious infection, I called my friends to reclaim their babes and drove them back to the farm. I knew I'd miss them and was especially concerned about Squeak's need for reassurance but I tried to take a reasonable approach: chickens can't live indoors and the house was surrounded by chicken-loving predators outdoors. After all, they had only been here temporarily....

A fortnight later I got a phone call: one of the chicks seemed very listless and wouldn't eat. I suspected constipation and arrived armed with mineral oil. It was Squeak. His appearance dismayed me—not only was he huddled and subdued, his toes were twisted back making it difficult for him to balance. He was much smaller than Bubble, his plumage was poor, his anus was encrusted with droppings and he looked most unhappy. Bubble, fortunately, looked fine.

I cleaned Squeak's bottom thoroughly with damp tissue, then tucked him into my shirt to prevent chilling. I hesitated about dosing him with mineral oil for constipation in case his condition was due instead to diarrhea. But when he still hadn't passed a dropping after forty minutes, I hesitated no longer and forced several drops down his throat with a syringe. Twenty minutes later he squirmed around quickly and shot an enormous gluti-nous mass down my front. Contrary to the reaction of someone respectable, I was elated. After a rest to recover, Squeak stood up looking bright-eyed and energetic. I set him down in the box beside Bubble and he began eating ravenously.

But something else caught my attention. Whenever a fresh dropping was produced, either chick would devour it instantly. This could only mean a dietary deficiency—probably protein since they were still eating only oatmeal and cornmeal. My friends were in a flurry of activities culminating in a family wed-ding and hadn't time to supply quantities of bugs as would a mother hen, so I offered to take back the chicks—temporarily; just till after the wedding.

Back again in my own home with the chicks, I pondered Squeak's twisted toes. Lack of frontal bracing caused him to lurch forward and backward repeatedly as he struggled for balance. In this state he'd never be able to roost normally. His toes were still very pliable so I decided to try straightening them. I cut a pair of corrective 'shoes' out of carpet underlay with grooves to hold each toe naturally aligned. Then I fitted each toe into its respective slot and pressed masking tape down on top to keep them in. Finally, I set him down and watched with amusement as he thumped his way around the box. Already his balancing had improved.

Eight days later I removed the shoes and Squeak, after having accustomed himself to lugging about large flat feet, found himself the possessor of small lightweight feet with straight slim toes. Over the ensuing months they regressed somewhat but never to as poor a state as originally. Perhaps a fortnight with shoes would have been ideal.

Squeak's inferior plumage was also a matter of great concern to me. He had a few stunted wing and tail feathers but his body was still downy, whereas Bubble was feathering out beautifully all over. Squeak's down, too, had been grown when his body was smaller and now fitted him sparsely, his pink skin clearly visible. Week after week passed without any noticeable change in his feather growth. The soiled down on his bottom fell away leaving skin that literally took weeks to become covered again.

At a painfully slow rate, feathers emerged down his front and underneath but over a two-month span. The new feather spikes down his back also took months to leaf out. In this prickly state he was extremely sensitive; being touched or handled, even gingerly, distressed him greatly. As his wing feathers finally began to lengthen, they too seemed extremely sensitive and often hung at awkward angles to his body instead of being tucked in tidily. His tail was the last to grow and, as a five-month old chicken, he still sported a ludicrous tuft of feathers that had been a sensible tail when he was a month old chick. It became increasingly clear throughout that cold wet autumn that Squeak, still staying 'temporarily,' would certainly perish if he were to return to the farm as an outdoor chicken.

In any case, he and Bubble were inseparable. So were we all, I was beginning to realize.

CHAPTER TWO
Hobbledehoys

As the chicks outgrew their box, I began leaving one side down so they could wander out to explore the house and yet return to feed or warm themselves under the brooder lamp. I placed a folded towel beside the woodstove and, whenever I lit a fire, the chicks lay on the towel, necks and legs outstretched, basking luxuriously. They quickly zeroed in on the kitchen as a great hunting ground for tantalizing tidbits and scurried around my feet in an excited blur at mealtimes. Besides the possible horror of spilling hot liquids or treading on them, I was electrified with anxiety whenever I inadvertently dropped chilli seeds or ground pepper onto the counter. If any were to fall on the floor, the speedier chicks would be on it before I could even twitch.

Besides sharing little portions of my supper with them, I'd cuddle them in my lap as I sat with my tea in the armchair. They'd follow closely at my heels and, as soon as I was seated, I'd lower my hand, palm up and perfectly horizontal, in front of Bubble who'd step daintily on while I 'elevatored' him up to my lap. Squeak, unfortunately lacking Bubble's perfect balance and confidence, would go rigid with fear and fall whenever I tried the same lift with him. So I'd scoop him up quickly, struggling and squeaking with anxiety, and cozy him down beside Bubble who was already settled and preening. Watching the two of them slumbering in my lap, warm and trusting, their downy innocence edged with light in the glow from the lamp, I would reflect sadly on the short tragic lives suffered by the majority of chickens— each intriguing personality, so charmingly individual, force-fed to ensure excessive growth and non-stop egg production, with brutal death as the culmination. And all according to prescribed government standards. Then as I gazed at the chicks still softly sleeping, their fragile beauty would blur into oblivion in my eyes.

Nap-time we all loved to share. If I lay down on the couch, both chicks would come scampering over and patter back and forth until I lifted them onto my chest. Then they'd snuggle down under my chin, preening and dozing and vying with each other to be closest to my face. One day they chose instead to lie down on my stomach as I drowsed. Within the soothing quietude of the room the fire hissed softly, the clock gently ticked and all was peaceful—until my stomach began to growl. At the first rumble, two round fuzzy heads on pencil-thin necks shot straight up, wide-eyed with adult vigilance. I stifled a giggle. Then *their* innards began gurgling too, and I began chuckling uncontrollably. As my body vibrated under them with every giggle, both chicks, with solemn dignity, sat with their heads revolving like chimney cowls, crops and stomach gurgling in unison. Perplexity and suspicion quivered in every feather while I heaved and laughed uproariously underneath them, pitching them about like little boats in a storm.

THE PROBLEM OF the chicks eating their droppings was resolved in short order by my cleaning up each dropping as it appeared and providing a highly varied diet; compared to mixed bugs and a wide range of human foods, droppings quickly lost their appeal. Moistened hard-boiled eggs from free-ranging poultry were particularly nourishing and satisfying. Soon, whenever Bubble and Squeak spied a dropping, they'd shake their heads firmly as though in disgust at earlier follies and walk away. This was delightfully humorous one day when I offered them a morsel of homemade halvah, a sort of fudge made from ground sesame seeds. I only realized what a fecal appearance it presented to them when they eyed it eagerly—then shook their heads simultaneously and stalked off.

Other foods, however, had tremendous appeal. Fresh tomatoes and chopped cucumber from the garden were an instant success, and in three days they devoured an entire fourteen-inch zucchini with unflagging zeal. Carrots were too hard to peck but carrot peelings became a favourite. Oddly enough potatoes, raw or cooked, were ignored. Apples remained an everlasting delight and porridge a favourite as long as it was served with milk. When the chicks were tiny, I ground their chick starter pellets and oyster shell grit in the blender, but as they grew into 'chicklets' this was no longer necessary. They quickly discovered the joys of home-made granola, shelled sunflower seeds, raisins, shredded coconut and muffins. 'Scratch,' a feedstore blend of oats, barley and cracked corn intended for poultry, they considered to be 'chicken feed' compared with wholefoods cookery. Truly they were chickens with discriminating palates.

SQUEAK'S DIFFICULTIES with balance and coordination waned gradually but clearly he'd never achieve normal roosting skills. Nor would he ever be able to sit in perfect stillness on top of my head like Bubble. Although he loved being cuddled, he was at least six months old before he lost his fear of the lift necessary to transport him up to my lap. His legs seemed to be inherently weak; not only was his walk somewhat stilted, but he lacked enough spring to jump. Instead he scurried about squeaking anxiously as Bubble basked in my lap, appropriating all my attention. Bubble quickly learned to make use of his wings to help his leap but Squeak's peculiar wings, jutting out at odd angles to his body, were more of a liability than an asset. When he lay down, they flopped out so far that Bubble often trod on them, igniting sudden shrieks from Squeak. They caused him such constant anxiety that even a slight touch would cause him to hitch them closer to himself with a petulant squeal. The lounge chair in the studio, being ten inches from the floor, was too high for Squeak so I placed a small box at the foot end as a step. He'd climb carefully onto the box and stand swaying from side to side with eyes eagerly measuring the leap. The he'd gather himself for the six-inch jump that would land him sprawling on the lounge where he'd lurch and slither his way along my legs to my lap, smug with triumph. Three months later he was at last able to dispense with the box and in time jumping became such pure delight that one morning he suddenly leapt gloriously from the lounge and bounced off my head as I sat at the easel bent over my work.

The indoor garden that had been the delight of robins in past years proved to be irresistible to the chicklets as they explored their small kingdom. Dustbathing became a high point of each day and they'd sprawl on their sides in ecstasy, throwing dirt up into their plumage. Sunlit shafts slanting through the clouds of dust amid the greenery had unmistakable charm but the gray film that clogged the leaves and crept like a tide over the furniture had less appeal. The finishing touch was when they'd step out of the garden and shake vigorously, depositing two impressive circles of excess dirt with a splay of toe prints in the centre showing the original colour of the floor. The great mystery to me was that dirt baths helped to maintain plumage just as beautifully as water baths. Another couple of shakes followed by contented preening and their feathers would positively glow with silkiness.

Eventually, I commandeered a large cardboard box, cut a doorway into the side, taped clear plastic sheeting across the top to illuminate the interior and restrict the dust, then layered the bottom with dirt. This arrangement, with occasional additions of fresh dirt, provided controlled dustbaths for the entire winter. However it became necessary to put green wire fencing around the indoor garden to convince the chicklets that my box idea was a subtle ultimatum, and also that the plants therein were not intended as their personal salad bar.

Night roosting for Bubble and Squeak presented another difficulty to be resolved. Due to the slow development of Squeak's plumage, I was obliged to leave a warm bulb on all night near him for so many months that by the time they were grown, both chickens still needed a nightlight. When I tried to bed them down without one, they panicked and ran about crying with fear. The light, in a sense, provided the comfort of a substitute mother hen and complete darkness was too much for them. Also, because Squeak's coordination was equally slow to develop, I couldn't supply a proper roost. Instead, they slept together on a large cushion beside the 'safety' of the light, Squeak nestled against Bubble's warmth. Bubble could have roosted normally at any time but I wanted him to help warm Squeak who was clearly a chicken with 'special needs.'

As THE CHICKS stretched up into gawky adolescents, their personalities continued to intrigue me. For some mysterious reason, they developed a passion for eating paper. A piece of newsprint or paper towel falling unheeded to the floor would be welcomed with shrill squawks of delight. If I didn't retrieve it immediately, they'd scratch it into shreds and devour it. They grew quite crafty at hooking books out of bookcases, rolls of paper towels off shelves, and magazines off tables. My recipe books, unthinkingly shelved at chicken-eye level, became an irresistible lodestone and were quickly deprived of covers and indexes. Whenever I was painting, Squeak would creep up silently, suddenly snatch a wadded paper towel out of my hand and scamper off clucking triumphantly, calling Bubble over to share the spoils. But whenever Bubble stalked my towel, I could always intercept him at the climax of his scheme since he couldn't restrain himself from low whispered clucks of anticipation as his beak reached out. Stuffing a paint-sodden towel into my jacket pocket failed to hoodwink them; long after I'd forgotten it was in there, either one of the chicklets, sitting in my lap while I worked, would suddenly hook it out and drop it down to the other and the chase was on. A guest leaving her purse on the floor had it ransacked for paper, and once I nearly lost a cheque to their insatiable lust. The day they discovered that some of the walls were covered with wallpaper was a black day indeed.

Most birds don't like being cuddled but Bubble and Squeak adored it, especially Squeak, and he developed a surprising degree of wiliness in extorting extra cuddles. Whenever I called them back into the studio to bed them down for the night, Bubble would follow me quite readily and tuck in happily to the 'nightcap' I'd provided on their cushion—a sprinkling of coconut, or

Bubble, a beautiful babe (above).

Squeak on an afghan (right).

Bubble and Squeak at the 'chicklet' stage (left).

Squeak with 'orthopedic shoes' (inset, bottom left).

Two hobbledehoys, Squeak (left) and Bubble (above).

Squeak sleeping (top). This photo inspired the linoprint Sleeping Sunrise *illustrated on page 11.*

A good shake after using the dust bath in the studio leaves behind only the footprints (above).

Squeak in my lap while I'm painting (left).

A sunlit Bubble (above).

A close-up Bubble (right).

Bubble and Squeak exploring the outdoors.

perhaps sunflower seeds. Squeak, however, having once lingered in the dining room until I returned and carried him out to join Bubble, craftily reinforced my 'training' by lingering each night till I came back, gathered him up and carried him out again. Those extra cuddles en route were well worth a little plotting beforehand. While I was painting, he'd tug at my pant leg till I reached down and stroked him with my free hand. And as I am right-handed, he invariably pulled on my left pant leg, knowing my left hand was free. When my concentration became fully reabsorbed by the canvas and my hand unconsciously stopped, he'd tug again for more. If he was particularly persistent, I'd sit him on my knee while I worked, and this gave him unutterable joy. His warm stillness and trusting companionship emphasized my immediate struggle to paint universal unity among all beings and gave an added poignancy to my efforts. In time I used Squeak in a linoprint entitled *Sleeping Sunrise* (illustrated) where inner illumination rising from below merges with his sleeping form (the rooster being the herald of the dawn). Above, a nocturnal moth of transforma-

Sleeping Sunrise, *linoprint.*

tion, composed of stars, moons and other images of the night, is absorbed by the growing light as Squeak sleeps on, trusting in the light's return, as must we all.

One day, being especially engrossed in my work and failing to respond appropriately to his tugs, he scratched loudly instead at the painting with his beak. In sudden consternation I laid a restraining hand on his back and admonished him gently. Then I patted him and resumed work. Of course Squeak had his own interpretation of my response; as soon as I withdrew my hand, he scratched the painting again. Only then did I realize that I had foolishly *rewarded* him. My only recourse was to endure Squeak repeatedly scratching the canvas and wait till he again tugged my pant leg before patting him again. Soon he did, and I instantly complied with unbounded enthusiasm; after testing the canvas method twice more, he reverted finally to the tried and true pant leg technique—much to my relief.

Squeak's insistence on monopolizing my attentions also betrayed an unmistakably jealous tinge. Whenever I was cuddling Bubble, Squeak would feign finding a choice tidbit on the floor and, picking it up and dropping it repeatedly, he'd cluck loudly and with such impelling excitement that Bubble, thoroughly distracted, would finally jump down to check it out—only to find nothing. Squeak's smug satisfaction as he'd take Bubble's place in my lap had to be seen to be believed. After falling for the ploy several times, Bubble chose finally to ignore Squeak in spite of his persistence.

In the studio lounge chair, when they were cuddled in a warm heap in my lap, Squeak insisted on being closest to me. As soon as I sat down, he'd leap into my lap in great excitement, then back to the floor and up into my lap over and over again, revelling in the exuberant hugs he earned on each re-arrival. Then he'd stand on my stomach with his face against mine, eyes closed, drowsing contentedly while I rubbed his neck feathers. Bubble, during these flamboyant sessions, bided his time roosting on my legs until Squeak finally simmered down and was sleeping in my lap. Then he'd pick his way carefully past Squeak and press his face softly against mine for his own special cuddling suited to his quieter, more dignified temperament. Only when Bubble, too, was satiated and lying down beside Squeak could I finally study the work on the easel—my original reason for sitting down. When we all headed out to the living room after a day in the studio, the two would run ahead and wait beside my chair, Squeak up on the footstool in excited anticipation.

As THEY GREW BIGGER and their faculties fully developed, Bubble and Squeak became aware of the richness of wild bird life on the other side of the windows. Feeding stations surround the house, resulting in a large, enthusiastic clientele year round. Although the chickens had hatched in early August, I was unable to take them outside until the following spring because of Squeak's defective plumage and the persistently cold wet autumn weather. Bubble, with greater nimbleness, was the first to gain the studio windowsills by way of a stool whereas Squeak, standing on the lounge chair, had to content himself with stretching up as tall as he could to see the outdoor activity. Not until he was nearly two years old did Squeak finally attain the windowsills on his own. Both would cower immediately in response to bluejay alarm calls, sometimes scuttling under the lounge to hide, and any large silhouettes flying overhead, particularly ravens, were carefully monitored with loud, raucous, warning calls that probably had hens for miles around scurrying for cover. Whenever the ravens flew over the roof out of the roosters' range of vision through their window, both heads would swing around to superintend the gradual disappearance of the airborne menace through the opposite window.

As their awareness increased, very little escaped their attention and I began dimly to understand how cocks, universal solar birds, came to symbolize vigilance in all directions. How natural now were the gilded roosters guarding churches from the vantage point of the steeples. Even a dulled thump from a neighbour's closing door would immediately arrest Bubble and Squeak's attention and illustrate the high standard of watchfulness inherent in roosters for protecting a flock of hens and chicks.

Reflections of this sort inevitably surfaced in art work. In an acrylic on paper entitled *Guardian of the Dawn,* Bubble looms tall in the darkness above while below his silhouette and within his breast, the sun of a new consciousness rises, protected and secure. Here, the sun is a Northwest Coast Sun Mask with wordless music pouring from the mouth, a plea for the illumination of ancient wisdom, a new awareness of cultural dignity reborn.

On rare occasions vigilance was relaxed, perhaps because it was my turn to be on guard. One drowsy afternoon I was lying back in the studio lounge with Bubble preening in my lap. I had set the chair at right angles to the windows so Squeak could clamber up my front to the windowsill and watch all the outside activity. Gradually we had all fallen asleep—I in my chair, Squeak on the windowsill behind my head, and Bubble in my lap, his head under his wing. Suddenly there was a terrific *BANG!* Shot out of oblivion, I found myself on my feet looking wildly about while both roosters crash-landed twelve feet away on the floor. I stumbled over to the window: a few barred feathers were plastered against the glass and a Sharp-shinned Hawk, looking dazed, was clinging woozily to a nearby branch, all hope of a chicken dinner obliterated from his mind!

With seed scattered for smaller birds beneath the trees surrounding the studio, periodic hawk attacks brought home to me the jarring transitions for prey from one level to another. Yet life is nourished by life, and a hawk's need of flesh is as legitimate as a grosbeak's need of seeds. Reflections on hawks led me to express them as thresholds to other realities.

In the print *The Great Dance,* the tree of life and death is composed of vibrating rhythms of myriad creatures all of whom must eventually pass through the dark shadow of the hovering hawk near the top. Above the hawk, transcendent spiritbirds are winging, a reminder that all of us must encounter the fearful shadow preceding the revelation of light.

In the print *The Coming of Darkness,* a radiant sun unfolds in birds of light while a swiftly swooping hawk, bearing darkness as a banner, reaches for the sun with outstretched talons: light is indivisible from darkness and the desire for one necessitates the acceptance of the other. The predator and the prey are one.

CHAPTER THREE

Predicaments and Predators

As THE COCKERELS MATURED, their plumage unfolded in beauty. Bubble rose out of golden downiness to become a huge, gorgeous red rooster with red-gold hackles and flank sickles and an elegant long, green iridescent tail. His feathers were so glossy that sunlit touches shone like sparkles on water. His eyes, dark in the beginning, moved through olive to orange colouring to match his plumage. His feet and legs became gracefully long and a dull olive while his beak had a black upper mandible and a yellow lower one.

Squeak, totally different and smaller, finally outgrew his silvery down for a wonderful creamy tweed tinged with russet—what I called his 'snowflake' plumage in that no two feathers were similar. Even shed feathers were replaced by dissimilar ones. His barred tail remained longer than a hen's but much shorter than Bubble's. His legs, curved toes, and beak were sunshine yellow but his eyes were the same orangey hue as Bubble's, without the contrasting 'eyeliner.' His plumage though, however beautiful, lacked the deep thickness of Bubble's so that his thinner, somewhat bony body was easily felt under the feathers. A wintry exposure would always be beyond him.

Both roosters grew immense red combs that curved heavily over to the left, and long, dignified red wattles. Their spurs grew continuously. In response to startled queries, I informed people that Bubble and Squeak were Great Crested Abyssinian Wonder Cocks—very rare birds indeed!

Soon another dimension came into play providing hours of amusement supplemented at times with intense frustration. I was alone in the kitchen one afternoon when I heard a sudden ghastly shriek from the studio. I tore out there, unthinkable horrors flooding my mind only to find both roosters looking up with placid curiosity as I scudded to a stop. Squeak lowered his head, braced himself and shrieked hideously. Then came the dawn of understanding: Squeak was learning to crow.

Thereafter, not only sunrise but any moment of the day or night was liable to be heralded at an ear-splitting register as Squeak practised crowing. Oddly enough Bubble, so much further advanced than Squeak in all other ways, waited another two months before his first discordant attempts. In a motley cacophany of squealing honks and hair-raising burbling screams, Bubble and Squeak untiringly proclaimed their adulthood that winter in one of the noisiest rites of passage it has ever been my misfortune to endure. The disadvantage of my early years in the city, rather than hardening me, had left me acutely sensitive to loud noise and I wondered dazedly in what strange, unforeseeable way this too would emerge in the artwork. The shattering impact of strident rooster calls erupting beside me as I tried to paint resulted in my quickly donning heavy-duty ear protectors similar to those used by men operating screaming chainsaws. The only difficulty with the ear protectors was that two roosters crowing indoors are louder than a mere chainsaw outdoors but at least I managed to hold my concentration. I strongly suspect that to Bubble and Squeak should go the dubious credit for certain images of shattered reality found in canvases that have been troubling the repose of curators ever since they were painted.

The difference in calls between the two roosters was humorous in the extreme: Squeak, physically unusual in every particular, had the classic, high-pitched call of the barnyard; Bubble, the typical red rooster of fable and nursery rhyme, warbled lugubriously like a drunken baritone. I began privately to call them 'Burble and Shriek.'

Eventually they reduced most of their crowing to the early morning hours unless visitors stopped in (which had to be announced to the world at large) or if the telephone rang. Squeak in particular developed an acute antipathy to the telephone. Whether I chose to dial out or merely answered an incoming call, he shrieked his disapproval in decibels that caused widespread mirth among acquaintances and utter disbelief during business calls with strangers. A call to a Toronto art supply store left the staff dissolving with laughter when receiving my order. Even hours after both roosters were bedded down in the darkened studio, Squeak's crows of annoyance would instantly ring out if the phone were used. Bubble knew I sat in my armchair when talking on the phone and plotted accordingly: whenever he heard me, he'd cunningly unlatch the studio half-door or simply sail over the top, to Squeak's outrage. Then he'd come running excitedly out to the living room, wings spread, feathers ballooning and leap, trumpeting with triumph, into my lap—to the great amusement, or confusion, of the caller. If the caller happened to be someone I couldn't avoid meeting later, my obvious embarrassment would spark off broad smiles between us.

Squeak eventually realized how deplorable I found his vocal achievements in close quarters and would often gather himself for a blast, hesitate on the brink as he watched me scrambling wildly for the headgear, then let it burst forth gloriously as I relaxed once again, ears thankfully protected. Then he began to manipulate extra cuddles by disgorging an ear-splitting shriek right beside me if I were hugging Bubble. As soon as I set Bubble down and gathered Squeak up into my arms, he'd cuddle down luxuriously in perfect silence. If all three of us were sitting together in my armchair in the living room and Squeak felt a sudden compulsion to crow, I'd set him down on the floor and motion him away firmly. Then he'd stalk into the dining room, get up on his own particular 'crowing stool' and get it all off his chest before rejoining us. It became an admirable arrangement.

Calling For The Light, *linoprint.*

In time, Squeak emerged in

a linoprint entitled *Calling For The Light* (illustrated) wherein energized sunrises of awakening pour from his open crowing beak while in the dark lower area of the print, waves like closed eyes symbolize the watery depths of our unconscious selves, still dreaming.

In an acrylic on paper called *Challenging the Darkness,* Bubble crows defiantly right and left at the darkness that embodies forms mysterious to our ordinary understanding, while multiple suns of illumination rise above.

After reaching adulthood, Bubble and Squeak still retained the wonderful rapport with each other that they'd enjoyed as chicks. Whenever I set a particularly succulent treat on the floor, the first rooster to pick it up would break out in a special guttural clucking of excitement. Holding the treat in his beak, he'd call the other over and give it to him. This was similar to a rooster calling his hens over for special tidbits except that Bubble and Squeak treated each other. The situation became particularly amusing when the recipient would in turn offer the treat back to the original giver who would again taste it, then offer it once more. By the time they'd finished passing it back and forth, there'd be so little left that finally one would capitulate and eat the remainder—to their mutual satisfaction.

However, whenever Bubble and Squeak disagreed, pseudo-cockfights would instantly erupt and they'd glower at each other, hackles raised and quivering, heads lowered, before leaping up with spurs foremost. Injuries were rare and were usually reduced to a minor cut on a comb. The winner was acknowledged when he stalked forward imperiously, head high, and the loser (invariably Squeak) lowered his head and turned it aside submissively; then peace would reign once more. However Squeak, ever one to persist, would bide his time until he could launch a sudden sneak attack on Bubble when his guard was down and jerk out a beakful of feathers. Bubble's retaliation would be so swift, though, that Squeak's elation at victory would be brief. There is 'room at the top' for only one rooster at a time.

Another entertaining aspect of Bubble and Squeak's maturity was the dawning of their chivalry towards me as though I were their hen. They'd greet my every appearance bowing and picking up tidbits and laying them at my feet. Even if I were only returning from another room in the house, certain formalities had to be respected and renewed. When one is hurriedly lugging a load of wash, yet is obliged to set it down in order to preserve the rituals of basic etiquette, one sometimes isn't as appreciative as one ought to be. Truly, our hasty lifestyle breeds discourtesy.

The cockerels also began to challenge visitors by lowering one wing and vibrating it against the 'off' foot while advancing sideways in a threatening posture. This produced a warning hiss somewhat reminiscent of an annoyed rattlesnake and proved intimidating enough to halt visitors dead in their tracks. Women and children were merely acknowledged as suspicious strangers but all roosters, human or otherwise, were definitely challenged. Their protection of me extended as far as responding to my distress calls as well: early one morning before I had let them out of the studio, I carried a steaming hot drink to my chair but lurched sleepily as I sat down, spilling scalding fluid straight into my lap. I shot up with a shriek. Instantly both roosters with loud thuds and answering squawks of alarm broke down the studio halfdoor and thundered out to the rescue.

BUBBLE AND SQUEAK'S first experience of the outdoors, so long delayed, finally occurred Easter Monday, a beautiful sunny day epitomizing the ultimate in spring weather. Gentle breezes stirred the crocuses and the welcoming earth seemed to smile and sigh happily in the growing warmth. I coaxed 'the boys' out the front door and down the steps, patting and encouraging them as they inched their way outside, their very combs tingling with trepidation and excitement. But it was the glory of damp earth under their toes that triggered their first joyous response and they immediately began scratching the dirt, turning up bugs and devouring them. The limitless sky overhead instead of a ceiling, and the presence of wild birds first hand instead of on the other side of a window, continually intrigued them. They were ever on the alert, eyeing rustling bushes suspiciously and warning each other about every shadow that passed overhead. Delighted as they were at this new world, their innate vigilance was redoubled. They followed me closely around the house showing an amusing blend of imprinting on me, fear in strange surroundings, and anxious protectiveness towards their 'hen,' gray and long in the tooth as she was. But the intensity of this new experience soon took its toll and after an hour-and-a-half they were exhausted. I led them stumbling with weariness back into the house where they fell sound asleep in my lap as I sat sipping herbal tea and gently caressing their feathers.

Much as Bubble and Squeak delighted in the natural world, I had many qualms about leaving them outside on their own. The house is surrounded by acres of woodland ceaselessly patrolled by original inhabitants like weasels and raccoons. Indeed, during several of our subsequent outings, one wispy raccoon in particular, drawn by the scattered birdseed under the feeders, lingered nearby hungrily watching the roosters. Only when I'd rush towards him waving a broom menacingly and shouting unmentionable epithets would he reluctantly vanish. Eventually I borrowed a large cage from a friend and began live-trapping the raccoons with a view to moving them out of the area. The only snag was that I lacked the strength (and nerve) necessary to carry an unwieldy cage filled with a lunging, snarling raccoon all the way down the path to my van. The friend proved to be gold; over the next few weeks twenty-one raccoons were transplanted by him in his car to chicken-free areas.

One of the difficulties about live-trapping is that one never knows who will be fuming inside the cage when one steps outside whistling in the morning. The first time I confronted an indignant skunk glowering at me through the bars, my blood froze in my veins. Then I hunted frantically for a prop and approached the cage warily, murmuring sweet nothings in a quavering voice which I hoped fervently would sound reassuring to skunk ears. The glaring inmate raised his tail threateningly as I drew near so I stopped instantly, but continued to mumble soothingly until he relaxed. Cautiously I reached forward, lifted the door slowly and wedged it with the prop before backing away carefully. Then I turned and fled to the house. From the window I watched the skunk creep forward, sniff suspiciously at the prop, then waddle past it to freedom. Once clear of the cage, his seething annoyance boiled over and he stormed up and down before the house quivering from end to end with the lust for revenge, tail straight up and ready for action. His hind feet barely touched the ground. For a full five minutes he fumed without avail before finally fading into the woods, tail erect and bristling with defiance to the very last. Fortunately, none of the other skunks I subsequently released ever sprayed me either. I had several living under the studio at the time and I began to catch them on such a regular basis that I'd have to awaken them once I'd propped open the door. Then they'd stagger out sleepily, stop for a scratch, and slither under the studio to doze away the day. One of them was quite distinctive: although he had white markings on his head and the tip of his tail, there were no familiar stripes down his back. 'Sooty' became such a frequent inmate that I merely stood aside after I'd opened the cage, chatting casually and yawning as he ambled slowly past to his den.

One night I was awakened by the most hair-raising cries outside. I lay rigid with horror until I could force myself downstairs to peek out the window. A large mother raccoon was ranging up and down before the cage in great distress with two babies at her heels. Inside the cage was a third baby. With increasing horror I began to fully realize my dilemma: should I venture outside to release the baby with an enraged mother ready to leap to its aid? Or should I stay safely inside fighting my conscience for the rest of the night? My decision was made immediately but it was nearly an hour before I managed to nerve myself to my duty, clad as I was in about six layers of protective clothing. Surprise seemed my best defense so I let out a bawl of defiance that wouldn't have fooled a dim-witted sheep as I burst open the door and clanged a saucepan. To my everlasting gratitude the mother raccoon fled, two tumbling babies in her wake. I leaped off the deck, jerked open the cage and scrambled back into the house tingling with relief. From the window, I raised a steaming hot cocoa and toasted the family's reunion as they disappeared together into the darkness.

As a result of the 'raccoon roundup' I was able to let Bubble and Squeak enjoy the outdoors on their own each day, cautiously reconnoitering the grounds each morning and bringing them inside well before dusk. Fortunately both roosters tended to stay close to the house by nature. As the afternoons grew hotter, they luxuriated in dustbaths side by side, leaving little double potholes wherever the dirt was choicest. When the immediate area around the house became firmly established as their own territory, occasional male human visitors found themselves at a severe disadvantage. Not only were they threatened, they would actually be attacked with spurs and beaks if they refused to retreat. Certain friends upon leaving the house found it wiser to back down the path keeping a wary eye on Bubble and Squeak who were determinedly escorting them off the premises. On the other hand, two little girls stopping in regularly for cookie handouts were never bothered. After all, not only were they 'chicks,' they were young 'hens.'

One day as I was busy indoors, I heard odd noises from the back of the house. Glancing out the kitchen window I was convulsed with merriment to see the man who annually delivered my firewood, a veritable two-hundred pound giant, pressed against the door and groping behind his back to knock. Bubble and Squeak, eyes cold with disfavour and deep suspicion registering in every raised feather, were at his feet holding him at bay.

Still, in spite of the roosters' growing confidence outside and the scarcity of raccoons, I watched over them closely, one part of my mind ever on the alert for their safety. I'd lost other birds to predators and such wounds never quite heal. When they finally came into the house for the night, I'd feel airborne from relief.

One afternoon when I was inside, I heard Squeak break out into shrill clucks of alarm. I hurled myself out the back door and spotted a huge hawk down on the patio. Squeak was only four feet away under the chokecherry bushes, squawking madly. I sprang forward and the hawk immediately took off. I snatched Squeak up in my arms but Bubble was nowhere to be seen. Then all rational thinking deserted me and I tore wildly around and around the house like a mad thing screaming "BUBBLE! BUBBLE!" Squeak, clutched in my iron grip, screeched hysterically. On the third lap, I suddenly spotted Bubble standing calmly under a bush watching the two of us with placid eyes as we hurtled by. My overwhelming relief at finding him safe was immediately eclipsed by the even greater relief that no one else had witnessed my brief frenzy. Restored reason assured me that no hawk could possibly get the magnificent Bubble off the ground; I could barely manage it myself.

CHAPTER FOUR
Doorstep Orphan

AROUND THE END OF MAY I received a phone call about a baby starling found literally on a doorstep one morning. The caller had been trying to care for him for a couple of days but now it was imperative to find someone else. Would I take him? An unnecessary question.

When he was delivered a short while later, the little creature, only a week old, was in a pitiable state. The previous 'godmother,' with perfectly good intentions, had been following the advice of a vet who should have known better, and feeding oily tuna cat food to the nestling. His droppings were entirely fluid from the excessively oily diet and his body thin and dehydrated. He also stank fishily. He gaped and cried with hunger as I held him on my lap, so I pushed an earthworm down his throat. Instantly he recognized 'real' food once more. Wolfing it down, he squealed shrilly for more and I added sowbugs and centipedes to the first course. When he was finally satiated and I had supplied a quantity approximating what a mother starling could hold in her beak for one feeding, he pushed himself along till he was close against me. Then he closed his eyes in rapture and fell sound asleep. 'Puck' had arrived.

The newest and smallest member of the family had the biggest mouth I'd ever seen on a nestling and had already been nicknamed 'Jaws.' His plumage was very sparse with new feather spikes pushing through his pink skin and large ridiculous tufts of down gracing the top of his head. His feet were enormous proportionately because they were already adult-sized and his diamond-bright eyes were unbelievably tiny. But it was Puck's appetite that really set him apart. I had never experienced anything so voracious. Ordinarily, I timed feedings at fifteen to twenty-minute intervals for week-old songbird nestlings but Puck would pipe up for more a mere seven minutes after I'd fed him. And it was distinctly a hunger call, not just the steady

'location' note regularly emitted by fledglings to maintain contact with foraging parents. As his insistence grew shriller each
time, I found I could hold him back only to ten-minute intervals
between meals with occasional lapses to fifteen minutes. He
began calling for food at dawn and ceased only at sunset when I
bedded him down on warm sweaters in a bucket and thankfully
draped a towel over the top. As I climbed numbly into bed and
closed my eyes, suddenly Puck would start up and it was already
sunrise—or so it seemed. This schedule called for nearly one
hundred meals a day. At two to three worms per feeding, or several sowbugs and centipedes, literally hundreds of mixed wrigglies
needed to be gathered each day—enough for at least two robin
nestlings, according to my previous experiences. I was constantly
haunted by the fear of overfeeding him, which is lethal, but he
thrived beautifully.

When the bug supplies were depleted in my own neighbourhood and I had to drive to other 'crawlier' areas, I took Puck with
me, since I'd be gone for several hours trying to build up a decent
supply. While I was digging, he'd be tucked into my shirt watching my every move. As soon as I'd spade up a big, succulent
worm, he'd squeak with eagerness. Then I'd pop it down his
throat and he'd burrow back inside to doze and digest. When his
bowels needed to move, he'd squirm around and push his rear out
of my shirt, wiggle it energetically, eject a lusty dropping and
scuttle back inside. Soon his tiny tufted head would reappear to
watch for the next meal.

This amusing manoeuvre was a great asset inside houses. As
soon as Puck wiggled his behind, pushing it over the edge of my
hand, or lap, or out of my shirt, I was forewarned and could
catch the squishy missile before it splattered onto any carpets—a
courtesy I never experienced during years of helping robin babies.
At the local gallery where Puck 'helped' hang an exhibit of paintings, the owner was definitely impressed with our teamwork. It
almost reconciled him to the large bucket of squirming wrigglies
dominating his desk.

Whenever I travelled with Puck, besides packing a prodigious supply of worms and mixed bugs, I would include his sleeping bucket. Then, when I needed both hands free, I'd tuck him inside on the sweaters and cover the top with a towel. Warm within the darkness, he'd sleep until hunger prodded him into squeaking for food. Starlings nest in tree holes or bird houses so Puck was very comfortable with this arrangement on a short-term basis. Like other babies, he still needed cuddling and reassurance as well as food. Weeks passed before a growing distaste for sleeping in the bucket each night overcame his trepidation and allowed him finally to roost like an adult. In contrast, young robins are out of the nest permanently by ten to twelve days of age, sometimes sooner. The differences between the two species never ceased to fascinate me, although I had no idea how typical a starling Puck was.

Bubble and Squeak's attitude to Puck was intriguing. I was curious to see how two mature roosters would react to a baby bird within their territory. Three days after his arrival I took a covered dish of mixed bugs out to the studio and settled down in the lounge chair, Puck asleep inside my jacket. Bubble and Squeak of course immediately jumped into my lap for cuddles and I patted them and rubbed their heads till they finally simmered down and began to preen quietly. At that moment Puck awoke and began to squeak for food. Both rooster heads, deeply engrossed in probing their plumage, instantly shot straight up. Then, as my jacket bobbed about and Puck suddenly peeked out, the roosters' eyes widened and their very combs quivered. I sneaked a worm out of the covered dish and dangled it invitingly over Puck who gobbled it down and squealed for more. The roosters leaned forward, fascinated. Their eyes, as they watched Puck's every move, were absolutely gentle, except for quick predatory gleams when they followed the progress of the worms. Squeak, who was closest, looked down at Puck with seemingly paternal, half-closed eyes. Both roosters quickly tuned in to the contents of the covered dish and although they made it perfectly clear that they were willing to empty it should the need arise, they also understood that it belonged to the babe and forebore to press the point.

Puck, on the other hand, was quite taken aback at these feathered whoppers towering above him. Although he faced them bravely, eyes transfixed, he shrank back into my jacket when they leaned down to peer at him, their heads, minus combs and wattles, about the size of his whole body. He didn't actually notice Desmond and Molly, the studio pigeons, until they suddenly thundered loudly past overhead. Then he immediately squirmed far back into my jacket and lay huddled under my armpit. This was definitely a world to be faced in easy stages.

For at least a fortnight after his arrival Puck familiarized himself with his strange new surroundings by peeking out warily from the dim safety of my jacket. I wondered if his eyes might be more sensitive to light than a baby robin's since, unlike them, his natural nestlinghood would take place in a dark tree hole. His strangely-ancient face contrasted comically with the billowy tufts of baby down glowing on top like sunlit dandelions gone to seed. Gradually he began to venture out into my hands or onto my lap, a wellspring of quickening curiosity urging him on. Whenever he tired, but was reluctant to miss all the activities around him, he'd wiggle down into my cupped hands as though into a warm nest and doze, rousing occasionally at puzzling sounds and blinking sleepily.

His first efforts to fly were surprisingly efficient, unlike the erratic blunderings of ten-day-old robins. But Puck by this time was two to three weeks of age with a half-grown tail for braking; newly-fledged robins are nearly tail-less. In devilishness too, he was easily ahead of comparable robin youngsters and his natural propensity for mischief accelerated alarmingly.

Weaning Puck from gaping for food to picking up his own was necessarily gradual—an amusing process studded with breakthroughs and backslidings as he oscillated between begging to be fed and demanding food to leap into his mouth. Sometimes his favourites, like halvah, would tease him mercilessly by their alluring, immobile proximity. With neck outstretched and beak wide open, he'd call and cajole repeatedly but the lump of halvah would stubbornly resist. Finally, as Puck inched closer and closer, his shrill cries would sound progressively less despairing until he'd suddenly seize the unwary halvah before it could escape. After a pause of astonishment at feeling it finally in his beak, he'd swallow it smugly.

Soon he was boldly thrusting his bill into folds of my clothing, prying them apart in the characteristic action of starlings seeking bugs in crevices. Before long he was probing curiously down into my ears or sorting through my hair. Then onto the table to lift up placemats. His beady bright eyes were situated directly at the base of his bill so that as it was pushed underneath something and opened, he was able immediately to see any hidden bugs. In quick order, he was parting the foliage in the garden and flicking open magazines on the table. However, one day an unexpected thrust between my lips just as I'd taken a mouthful of hot tea shot a sudden cascade down my front and unleashed a flash flood of muttered invective against all starlings ever hatched.

The roosters, too, came in for their full share of Puck's impishness as he strutted around on their backs prying unceremoniously under their feathers and tugging on them sharply. He'd perch on their toes, unconcernedly dwarfed by their hugeness, reach up and impudently jerk their wattles when they leaned down. At times he'd zoom over and bounce down abruptly on Squeak's back as he slumbered with his head under his wing; Squeak wouldn't even open an eye. I marvelled at the dignified forbearance of these roosters. Puck's interest in prying open my own eyes I firmly discouraged and no one who has yet to experience it can possibly imagine the excruciation of an unsuspecting nostril being suddenly twisted wide open by a piercingly sharp beak. That he rarely, if ever, found a bug on me failed to discourage him from minutely searching, not only my person, but that of anyone foolhardy enough to visit. Ritual words of welcome mingled with amusing speculations on personal standards of hygiene as Puck rooted determinedly through each visitor's hair and peered brazenly underneath their clothing.

When he was still being handfed, Puck hadn't needed to drink, the moisture in the bugs being sufficient—especially as I occasionally dipped them into water. But as he became mobile, I tried to coax him into drinking still water in a small dish. Our first efforts weren't successful but as I was rinsing out a large, flat bathing dish for him, he became immediately excited about *running* water. In a flash he had jumped down into the dish, so I steadied it and let it fill to overflowing. Within moments Puck's wings were a watery blur as he thrashed happily, soaking us both. After that aquatic crescendo, mere drinking came quite easily.

Puck's first bath also ushered in the most passionate craze for water that I'd ever seen in a bird that wasn't a duck. When I watered individual plants he became instantly excited and bobbed in and out of them, probing into the wet earth and roots, and trailing me enthusiastically from pot to pot. Whenever I sprinkled the indoor garden, he'd scamper under the dripping leaves and prod through the mud. Once, an elderly visitor, whose experiences with birds were limited to caged budgies, sat transfixed at lunch as Puck ingeniously contrived a thorough bath in her glass of water, showering her liberally in the process. Be it ever to her credit that her reaction resembled the spontaneous delight of a child at a birthday party. In spite of my greater exposure to the antics of birds, I found myself one fine day unable to convince Puck that the hot strawberry jam I was stirring beneath billowing clouds of steam was *not* bath water. His manic persistence drove me to desperate contortions as I tried futilely to stir jam without first raising the lid on the pot.

The supreme joy of water churning and sloshing during laundry sessions threw him into such ecstacies that I didn't dare take my eyes off him for a moment. He was blithely untroubled by fear and leaped right down onto the clothes in the machine. As the water steadily rose, he pried into wet folds and paddled in the widening pools, chattering incessantly. I quickly gave up worrying about the chemical breakdown of soap and its possible effects on starlings; it was all I could do to get him safely out long enough to shut the lid. When the cycle finished and I began transferring wet clothes into the adjoining spindryer, Puck rode gaily on top of them and climbed straight in, bubbling with inexhaustible curiosity. Even the roar of the whirling machine as he stood on top of it failed to daunt him; on the contrary, he whistled and sang all the louder. His sense of security was untouchable—for which I heartily envied him. When the hazards of doing the laundry were again safely surmounted, I felt as if I'd been through the wringer myself.

Activities involving the kitchen tap attracted Puck immediately and he'd scramble along my arm, bill outstretched for a drink as soon as he heard the water flowing. Filling the kettle became a perpetual challenge with Puck not only monopolizing the water but craftily flicking the cover down over the spout while it was still filling and consequently spraying us both with the deflected flow. He shared every shower with me, sitting on the curtain rod or on my head under the spray and ever singing joyously. When I shut off the tap, he'd hop down into the tub to chase trickles of water or to pry my toes apart with excruciating dexterity, seeking hidden droplets. If I happened to wash my hair under the kitchen faucet, my scrubbing fingers would be constantly entangling with Puck's toes and getting rapped reprovingly with his razor-sharp bill. Protecting his probing bill from scalding mugs of herbal tea became a daily occurrence and resigning myself to his insistent baths in my mug as soon as the tea was an acceptable temperature, a humorous inevitability. I began seriously to wonder if that devilish starling plumage could possibly disguise a reincarnated duck.

Even the pigeons could touch off Puck's water fuse. He'd be instantly intrigued as they bathed in their pedestal birdbath, sluicing water out in glittering arcs or basking blissfully while I showered them with a plant mister. As the water dripped steadily onto the floor below, Puck would be so excited that he'd jump into the roosters' water dish for an exuberant splashing. I soon found it impossible to maintain clean water for Bubble and Squeak; when I filled their dish each morning, Puck would ride on the rim out to the studio where he'd immediately plunge in for his first bath of the day. Subsequent baths would commonly occur in the pigeons' small water dishes despite the yellowy tint of dissolved vitamin powder.

Bubble and Squeak, of course, were wholly unmoved by all this aquatic excitement. They firmly upheld the superior virtues of dustbathing.

In the print The Quickening Thaw (detail),
*our human nature, frozen into terrestrial
concerns, is yet capable of thawing and releasing
the flow of new beginnings, symbolized by the
eager-eyed nestlings, like Puck.*

CHAPTER FIVE

Summer Highlights

AT THIS POINT, I decided to reintroduce Puck to the natural world. All his activities showed great dexterity—perhaps too much at times. Though I was still replenishing the bug box for him, he was wholly in charge of his own feedings. With his ever-prying beak ceaselessly rooting through the house for any unwary bugs, I felt that now he should find his own food outdoors.

But Puck had other ideas.

Once out of the house, he glanced at the wild birds nearby, some of whom were starlings; he peered up at the dazzling sky above, and at the sunlight sparkling on the leaves; he very likely spotted multitudes of insects that escaped my inferior eyesight, but he was back in the house before I was. Puck had no intention of relinquishing the luxurious life of a cosseted indoor starling.

Puck's adolescence will live forever in the minds of those who were unwitting victims of it. He was sauciness incarnate. At the slightest thwarting of his will, his head feathers would swell out defiantly and he'd hammer frenziedly on unsuspecting hands with his knife-like bill. Concerned fingers cautiously removing a scald-ing hot tea bag from his curious, outstretched beak would be immediately targeted. My attempt to snatch a straight pin from his grasp would throw him into a tantrum. Preventing him from imbibing wine, poking his beak into an electric toaster, landing on a hot frying pan, tasting diced jalapeno peppers—all were annoying interferences and his temper would instantly blaze up. The very movement of fingers near him would so irritate him that he'd deal out several sharp raps of reproof if I even twitched while he dozed on my hand. Food had to be presented with minimal motion.

Months later, I noticed a visitor being rapped on his fingers as he offered bits of halvah to a bristling Puck, head feathers at their cockiest, who was snatching up the morsels between tantrums. With almost a shock, I realized that I couldn't recall when Puck had last hammered my own fingers—obviously, I'd been 'trained.' But the subtle differences in my more acceptable movements were so naturally carried out that I was unable to coach anyone else in what not to do!

IN CONTRAST to his outlandish sauciness, Puck had his gentler side and he never lost his love of snuggling inside my shirt and dozing there, cozy and warm. If he wasn't sleeping, he'd just nestle down, his tiny star-bright eyes blinking at me drowsily. Although he wouldn't tolerate fingers, perhaps warned by ancestral memory, he enjoyed my face touching him. After a few months of watching me patting and hugging the roosters, he began pressing himself against my face whenever Bubble and Squeak basked in my lap. Soon I understood that he wanted to be included too, and I'd rub his feathers with my face, murmuring to him affectionately. Before long he was jealously devising ploys to distract my attentions from the roosters to himself at every sitting. Other times, being the most irrepressible of starlings, he'd pop out of my shirt long enough to tweak their combs or wattles and devilishly rouse them up. Then he'd scuttle back to his lair, safe and gleeful. I'd avenge the roosters by poking through my shirt at Puck, rapidly and at a different spot each time, while he dodged around inside trying to grab my finger.

'Hidey-holes' were the norm for Puck—dim enclosures in which he felt very secure, a natural carry-over perhaps from nestlinghood in a treehole with the family. As soon as dawn lightened the darkness of the house, he'd swoop up the stairwell from his roost in the studio and land on my bed. With tiny high squeaks of welcome, he'd run eagerly up to my face and start prying under the covers. I'd take the hint and, with a drowsy dexterity that improved daily, prop the covers into a small tent with a tiny doorway. Puck would immediately push his way inside, chattering continually, and pry under the entire perimeter of the tent edges. Satisfied finally, he'd cozy down in the warm darkness, preen awhile and doze. Later, he often lay on the side of my neck while I hovered between yielding to the urge for more sleep, and lying still with closed eyes, delighting in the feel of his feathery warmth against my skin. Our early morning rendezvous soon became so special to me that whenever I woke in the predawn darkness, I'd wait for the light to bring Puck before I'd rise.

Hidey-holes also meant safety. Whenever Puck took fright spotting a hawk nearby or reacting to a sudden outbreak of blue-jay alarm calls, he'd zoom into my shirt. If it wasn't open, he'd land on the back of my neck and crouch in hiding behind my head as I peered out of the windows seeking the cause. Once, during a general panic, I came into the studio just as he shot into Molly's box, her inner sanctum, where she'd lie in the dim interior cooing to herself. As luck would have it, Molly chanced to be 'home' and a sudden, thumping free-for-all erupted. Amid an uproar of squawks and outraged coos, Puck shot out as fast as he'd gone in. I decided Puck needed his own 'storm shelter' and set up a small box with a folded washcloth inside and a starling-sized circular door. There, during times of rest, Puck would often lie just inside the entrance, his drowsy eyes watching me as I worked.

IN MIDSUMMER I began to notice a problem with Squeak's ears. The stiff feathering covering the ear holes looked dark and sticky, and he scratched at his ears far too frequently. When they began to smell strongly, I realized there was definitely a problem, my guess being ear mites. Probing under the feathers, I discovered both ear holes full of a yellowy paste. Each day I cleaned them thoroughly with cotton swab sticks dipped in hydrogen peroxide. However, after two weeks of this treatment, Squeak was still scratching at his ears, manipulating his throat as though the itching were inside, and shaking his head each time. Baffled, I decided to have a swab analyzed by the vet and since the roosters were inseparable, I piled them both into the van.

As we started off, they found the roar of the engine and the bumping, swaying motions terribly disconcerting and lurched nervously along the floor towards me. I tried to reassure them over the noise and patted them constantly but they still eyed the whizzing landscape through the windows with mounting apprehension. Finally Squeak took advantage of a pause at a crossroads to leap into my lap with flailing wings just as I accelerated. In a moment Bubble had followed suit and I truly had my arms full as I strained to maintain my own side of the highway while peering between their bobbing heads. The steering wheel seriously diminished the size of my lap and both roosters scrambled wildly for solid footing while I prayed that the Mounties wouldn't be as vigilant as usual. In grand state we finally drove through the town streets amid the incredulous stares and swivelling heads of pedestrians, and the erratic swerving of oncoming drivers who could see only roosters at the steering wheel. With a massive sigh of relief, I turned into the yard of the veterinary clinic—surely a place where nothing could ever seem unusual to anyone.

How wrong I was.

I gave both roosters a reassuring cuddle, detached Bubble firmly and carried Squeak inside. In the first chair a woman sat with a small dog on her lap; in the second was a young boy with a cat in a travelling cage on his lap. I took the third chair. Behind the counter, two women were busy dealing with never-ending accounts and phone calls, and funnelling clients into the examining rooms. But a sudden hush had fallen and I looked up: all eyes were fastened on the third chair where I sat. It had gradually dawned on them that I was holding a rooster in my lap—a first for the clinic.

In the outbreak of bantering and merriment that followed, Squeak quickly became the star attraction. His confidence, at a shaky low from the ride in, soared to unprecedented heights as everyone patted him and fawned shamelessly over him. Soon he was crowing gloriously, his eyes beaming in the glow of universal admiration while I noted grimly that my ears were the only ones that winced. When I carried him, smug with triumph, into the back room to be examined, four excited female employees trooped after us, chattering jovially. A local power outtage provided

further gratification for Squeak since, in the darkness of the win-
dowless room, one of the women was obliged to direct a back-up
spotlight on him—the crowning touch.

Later, when I carried him back out to the van where Bubble
was waiting disconsolately, everyone else came as well, even a
newly-arrived female client. This time Bubble, too, was petted
and pampered, a gloating centre of lavish feminine adulation, and
I was actually thanked for coming, before I drove away. The final
eye-opener was the tasteless complacency of both roosters on the
way home as they ignored my now needless reassurances—they
might have been royalty disdaining to fraternize with a paid driver.

Hours later, when I bedded them down for the night, they
were still strutting and beaming—with true male arrogance!

The vet had dissuaded me from the expense of an analyzed
swab, feeling certain that a variant of yeast in the ear canal was
the culprit. For a week, I dutifully cleaned Squeak's ears each day,
which he tolerated good-naturedly, and added a trickle of ear
drops, which he loathed. Then a few days respite followed by
another week of treatment. I sensed a mild improvement but the
condition gradually regressed and I decided to press for an analysis.

So off we drove to the vet clinic again.

This time, no doubt with the remembrance of their previous
triumph still lingering in their memories, the roosters were
delighted to get into the van. Bubble rode on the passenger seat
admiring the view while Squeak insisted on sharing my lap with
the steering wheel. Both of them positively purred with enjoyment. Again, rounded eyes of disbelief clung to us as we manoeu-
vred through the bustling town streets and when I carried Squeak
into the waiting room we were met with cries of welcome.
Indeed, an older woman who had brought her cat seemed unable
to detach her astonished eyes from Squeak. Though a farm
woman all her life, she'd never seen a rooster basking contentedly
in anyone's lap, much less patted one.

A different vet advised me to stop using the somewhat abra-
sive hydrogen peroxide and to switch to mineral oil for cleansing.

This was excellent advice and I began to see an improvement within the next few days as the irritation subsided. The analysis, in confirmation, showed normal bacteria and no mites. But Squeak's ears for years would always produce hard balls of compressed dirt and wax which had to be removed weekly with forceps.

This time the return trip had a new twist. As I drew near home, I spotted a hunter in glaring safety-orange clothing preparing to stalk into my woods. I pulled alongside and hailed him. He sauntered over nonchalantly, a tinge of contempt on his unwashed face, his rifle swinging precariously, and stared in at me moodily.

Masking my disgust for pleasure killing with a veil of cheery tactfulness that deceived neither of us, I smiled and stated firmly that no hunting was permitted on this property.

"There's no signs," he growled, predictably.

"There *are* signs," I replied lightly and added with devastating logic, "perhaps you missed them." I withheld the reflection that it's easy to miss what one doesn't want to see.

A subtle change had been creeping over his unshaven face. It was as sullen as ever, but his eyes now held a note of mockery. As I added the inevitable observation on the weather, followed by a polite comment to the effect that he take his lust for blood elsewhere, he was obviously suppressing a hearty guffaw. I drove home simmering. "Such arrogance!" I fumed, "just laughing up his sleeve at me."

Later, I remembered that I'd had two enormous roosters wedged cozily into my lap, hopelessly undermining my dignity. In retrospect, I couldn't help but admire the man's reticence.

ABOUT THIS TIME, a couple arrived at the door with a cage containing a panicky female robin. They had rescued her from one of the busiest streets in town and she was unable to fly. It was mid-July and I was instantly concerned that she might have eggs or babies in hand. But when I looked into her eyes, I had an immediate sense that she was between clutches. In no way could I prove my reading but I was certain that it was so.

I reached into the cage, gathered her into my hands and drew her out. As I held her close to me checking for any obvious injuries, she pressed herself against my front, closed her eyes and relaxed completely. Such a pure gesture of trust from a wild adult was overwhelming. After sleeping in my hands for more than an hour while I sat quietly in the living room, 'Missy' finally opened her eyes. Then she moved about restlessly, dropped down clumsily to the floor and hopped out to the screened porch that was to be her home indefinitely.

There was no doubt that she was unable to fly, although both wings moved normally, so I felt she had probably suffered a severe bruising from a passing car. She responded well to offerings of mealworms, berries, mixed bugs and water, and passed normal droppings so I hoped that, once again, time would prove the great healer.

Each day, I swept the fields for insects with my pillowslip net and Missy quickly understood that the huge inverted bag shaking insects onto the table in front of her was not to be feared. As darkness came on, she would become uneasy about sleeping in the porch and would hop through the unlit living room to my chair, mount level by level to the top and roost quietly there for the night. I helped to ease her trepidation about entering the house by leaving the lights off in her immediate vicinity and making myself scarce. Once she was asleep on the chair, I'd glide through the darkness to the door, quickly latch it, and fade away to the other side of the house. In the morning, I'd open the door while the growing light was still dim, in readiness for her. We had an excellent arrangement.

One morning about a week after she'd come, I was late coming downstairs. When I did descend, yawning, I passed Missy just hopping back calmly from the studio on a tour of inspection. Her unique blend of trust and reserve was undeniably conducive to the healing process.

Puck and Missy shared the premises well except for three or four occasions when Puck suddenly trounced her briefly—

perhaps territorially, or out of pure devilment. He conveniently reinforced her limited trust in me by perpetually climbing all over me, no doubt to her mute astonishment. Missy, on the other hand, taught Puck how to pound and eat beetles, a gourmet skill I've never developed.

Ten days after her arrival, Missy was making her first tentative flights, and in two weeks was swooping from screen to screen with true robin finesse. Sixteen days after she'd come, frightened and flightless, I opened the screen door and watched with utter delight as she lifted effortlessly up into the trees. Then I knelt down, looking up at her and seeing her own evident delight in her recovered health and freedom. Moments like these are to be savoured.

Later that evening, I leaned back with a lap overflowing with warm, sleepy chickens and Puck snuggled under my shirt. I gently slid my fingers through Squeak's beautiful handwoven-like plumage, the silky feathers rippling with fluid grace. His eyes were totally closed except when he'd part them a fraction to peer up at me, his whole facial expression resonating enjoyment. Beside him Bubble drowsed deeply, eyes closed, his long iridescent tail feathers flowing over the chair's edge in complete relaxation. Deep snores rose occasionally as they slumbered, oblivious of the world around them. Inside my shirt, Puck dozed contentedly, his tiny, star-bright eyes peeking out at me at rare intervals.

I rested my head on the back of the chair and ruminated on these two species—one considered to be more of a joke than a type of creature with personality and dignity, fully entitled to fulfil their own potential; a species abused daily in unspeakable ways, whose defeathered bodies are wrapped in plastic, barcoded and slung into grocery bins.

The other species has been cursed for not being native to this country (how few of us can claim that privilege!) and, although introduced by humans, are now disparaged for possessing similar 'go-getting' instincts. However, they are as native to this country now as we are.

I gazed, too, at the pigeons asleep above me on their lofts—another species considered purely as a nuisance, if considered at all—and abused by fancy breeders for their own competitive ends.

Truly, all five birds trustfully at rest around me, with their intricate personalities ever unfolding, are generally considered to be unworthy of human empathy.

My thoughts then wandered to the miracle of Missy's recovery. Where in the darkening woods was she roosting now?

CHAPTER SIX
A Comedy of Errors

I HUNG UP THE TELEPHONE IN A GLOW. Company coming soon; lifelong friends from another province who hadn't come East in years. I sat back in my chair happily absorbed in delightful anticipations—until I opened my eyes and scanned my surroundings: the dinginess of aging painted walls; chewed wallpaper at chicken-beak level; the huge, haphazard heap of fresh garden veggies in a trail of dirt upon the table; the monstrous roll of new turf carpeting (suitable for tender avian toes and a warranted match for adhesive droppings); the now opaque windows overlooking feeders, and begrimed nightly by muddy raccoon paws; the hanging lamp above the diningroom table with its paper globe shade shredded into dreary tatters—one of Puck's contributions.

I shuddered. Truly, cleansing power of industrial strength would be necessary to prevent the premises from being publicly condemned. With visitors on the way, the sooner I began the transformation, the better.

The veggies were an obvious priority. With alluring visions of frozen, pre-cooked meals ready to serve, I waded through mounds of beans, peas, zucchini, onions, carrots, potatoes and chard in a frenzy of washing, slicing, chopping and steaming. Puck, wildly enthusiastic, was in his element grabbing at the knife as it sliced, snatching peas out of their shells with incredible quickness and swooping far too close to jets of steam escaping from under saucepan lids for my peace of mind. The frenzy of his wings when he slipped into a bowl of flour shot a flurry of dust over the entire counter and ignited miniature sparks on the hot electric burners. Chopped beans began to appear mysteriously on living room windowsills and when he knocked a light plastic bowl full of dirt and compost cuttings all over the kitchen floor, I reminded myself gratefully that the visitors were still three provinces away.

Manoeuvring cooked meals into the freezer presented an

almost insuperable challenge due to Puck's inability to resist puncturing plastic bags. I had long since relinquished saving them for re-use but would drop the riddled remains resignedly into the recycling depot instead. Meanwhile, although I kept newly-sealed bags of food covered with a thick towel while I filled the next ones, as soon as my eye was off him, he'd lever up the towel and thrust his beak triumphantly through a bag. Then I'd have to transfer the contents quickly to another before they oozed all over the rest. Even riding shotgun over them to the freezer failed to guarantee their safety. Puck would spring fearlessly into the upright freezer and climb over the frozen packages seeking fresh ones to puncture while I shooed him fruitlessly with one arm and juggled a slithery load of 'targets' with the other. After two days of such calculated culinary harassment, I almost longed to dine out for a week.

From the kitchen, Puck and I progressed to repainting walls, another unending challenge as he taxed his ingenuity with ways of getting into the latex paint and I taxed what was left of mine with ways of thwarting him. His tantrums whenever I drove him away from the paint bucket sent him whirling defiantly around and around my gesticulating brush while splatters of paint flew merrily. A big drop hitting the floor ignited us like a hockey puck dropped between two players as we both hurled ourselves on it— me, to wipe it up, and Puck, because he knew I didn't want him to touch it. His relentless persistence in pursuing whatever he sensed to be forbidden territory was uncanny—and exhausting. Our follow-up project of laying turf carpeting down in the livingroom was accomplished with Puck dashing at the snipping shears and my hair standing permanently on end. Wallpapering became a Sisyphean task as I pressed each panel flat to the wall at one end and Puck pried it up at the other. Periodically, he'd tire of all the activity, being a youngster still, and would fall sound asleep, endearingly but rather inconveniently, on my arm or shoulder. Then would I begin to sympathize with the plight of the oft-quoted 'one-armed paperhanger!'

As the deadline for the visit drew nearer, the house (in some parts) began to show definite improvement, although I pondered uneasily an outsider's reaction to some of our 'norms.' One of Puck's favourite amusements was his 'log-rolling act' on the roll of toilet paper which tended to shred rapidly as it whirled round and around under his scrambling claws. Somehow I felt that not everyone could adapt easily to the inferior absorbant quality of limp tatters that dangled uninvitingly from the roll. Molly, too, had a daily habit of ensconcing herself under the tub, cooing contentedly in the darkness. Anyone using the facilities violated her privacy and she'd glide out, silently and unseen, to fasten her beak suddenly on an unsuspecting ankle, beating the victim's legs with her wings for emphasis, and cooing irritably. Desmond, not to be outdone, would, as likely as not, be roosting on top of the door, preventing its closing and banishing any pretensions to modesty or privacy. The big rock inside the bathtub, situated to deter weasels from emerging from the drain, would be bound to cause comment amongst city-dwellers. Finally, should anyone step out intact from the bathroom, Bubble, reaching saucily through the tiny pigeon door opposite, which is cut into the larger studio door, would nip them speedily on the toes, unless the visitor was even speedier. Somehow, I strongly suspected that the crumbling outhouse with its attendant horrors of scuttling spiders and matted cobwebs would prove more alluring to the less adventurous-minded than the indoor bathroom with its nefarious denizens lying in wait.

The shredded lampshade problem I had resolved adroitly by replacing it with a solid, handmade, stained-glass shade—a defiant answer unchallenged as yet by Puck. Another priority was a couch cover of denser weave than the frayed blanket that had served to date. Puck, prying apart the fibres, had discovered hidden cushions below and each day saw long fringes from the cushions hooked out through the blanket and standing up gaily in a random pattern of tufts all over the back of the couch. I began to realize the necessity of being threatened periodically by an influx of visitors just to goad me into maintaining some veneer of normality in my daily living arrangements.

With only a few days remaining, I plunged into the studio to give it a thorough scouring and Puck 'helped' by riding on my feet as I swept up seeds and droppings. Pigeon lofts and rooster territories were scrubbed, in spite of protests, and windows washed till they shone. But when I dragged out the vacuum cleaner, Puck hid among the stored canvases behind the dust curtain till the hideous roar was finished. I concluded that it was the snaky action of the hose that unnerved him since the equally horrendous roar of the blender merely caused him to burst into song—something it has never done for me.

At this critical juncture, my ancient refrigerator gave up the ghost and I was in a near panic to get a new one delivered in time. As soon as it finally arrived, Puck seized every opportunity to climb all over the gleaming 'junglebars' inside while I puzzled over just why this new fridge had such charisma. Then I remembered that the old one had lacked a workable inside light. No wonder that this bright interior with every item aglow was so intriguing. The new fridge was also louder than the old one, and each time the cycle switched on, both Puck and the roosters would jerk up their heads, startled. But in time, the disruptions went unnoticed.

Doing the final laundry was the usual wild scramble with the added bonus of Puck balancing with consummate skill on the indoor drying line for a nap and loosing droppings at regular intervals down the clean sheets before I noticed the suspicious lull in our activities and traced out the cause.

However, the night before the guests were due to arrive, all was in readiness—barring a huge canvas leaning against the wall but due for pickup first thing in the morning. Thankfully, I heated frozen homemade soup, too weary to attempt anything more challenging and loath to create further mess. Every muscle pleaded to lie down and I leaned against the counter eating my soup, too tired to walk to a chair. My mind was still tense and buzzing as I mentally checked and rechecked my preparations for any glaring omissions. At this moment, determined to penetrate my preoccupation, Puck thrust his beak deep into my ear and pried it apart with an excruciating twist. With convulsive spontaneity, I jerked a full soupspoon at him which strewed part of its contents across the clean floor and splattered the rest against the canvas. Needless to say, I totally missed Puck who had shot away the instant I howled. With bellowed threats about his near future in which a stuffing flavoured with sage and onion figured prominently, I mopped the floor and canvas clean and stumbled off to bed.

THE GREAT DAY dawned bright with anticipation as I drowsed luxuriously in bed, Puck nestled angelically on the side of my neck in an aura of innocence that fooled no one. This cynical observation was quickly confirmed by his defecating with premeditated dexterity directly into my clean underwear just as I reached out for it. Breakfast was even more of a circus than usual when Puck suddenly stuck his toes under the breadknife as I was preparing to slice, shooting me into the last throes of anxiety before I was even fully awake. He quickly followed up his advantage by paddling in the honey on my toast and tracking its sweet stickiness all over the scoured windowsills. Then, while I warded him away from my food, he climbed up the cord of the electric kettle as it was heating and poked his beak curiously into the spare socket. My sudden leap to deflect him from possibly electrocuting himself knocked my toast and honey onto the clean floor and the day was under way.

Giving up the unequal struggle to have a quiet breakfast, I went out to the studio where morning light was pouring through a faceted glass suncatcher. There I discovered Bubble trying to pick up a tiny rainbow from the floor—one of those priceless moments that are the joy of living with birds. I let the roosters outside and began my daily cleaning of waterdishes and droppings, my tensions mounting feverishly between the anxieties of preparation and anticipation. Thinking that a little music might soothe my frayed nerves, I turned back to play a new tape I'd borrowed, only to discover with unspeakable horror that Puck was happily disgorging it from the cassette holder. It trailed to the floor in undulating loops and twists. Shooing him away agitatedly, I spent the next ten minutes painstakingly reeling the unbroken tape back into the cassette before locking it away with a sigh of relief. When I returned to the studio to continue the still unfinished chores, I found Puck just ending a bath in Molly's water dish, the yellowy splotches of vitamin-enriched water trickling down a newly-primed canvas and dripping onto the clean floor.

When the visitors were nearly due, I trudged upstairs to change into clean clothes and Puck swooped up the stairwell behind me to 'help.' Then I spotted a massive spider, thanked my lucky stars that it would be gone before the guests arrived, and pointed it out to Puck. He was very excited and pounced it several times rather nervously but lacked the experience to incapacitate such a monster yet. So I grimly performed that task for him and left him dismembering and swallowing the remains with every evidence of enjoyment while I dressed. But as I stood before the mirror, one eye on the clock and buttoning my nice new blouse for the occasion, Puck, looking very uneasy, landed on my shoulder and vomited the entire spidery mess down the back of my neck.

I greeted my visitors in an unironed sweatshirt, the greenish pallor of my face fixed into a grim smile of welcome and my hitherto vegetarian mind toying with visions of cooked starling for supper!

CHAPTER SEVEN

Before the Snow Flies

THE SUMMER HEAT AND HUMIDITY MERCIFULLY WANED, giving way to cool fresh mornings with touches of orange and gold brightening the surrounding hills. The unmistakable smoky tang of autumn was in the air as woodstoves were kindled more frequently. Circling and soaring, each flock of fledglings and adults moved as one bird in quickening anticipation of the great journey before them. As the nights grew frostier, both the falling leaves and the flying birds would begin their migrations to other realities.

With winter approaching, I began to focus on the heavier jobs on my schedule. An enormous pile of split hardwood had been delivered and dumped in the pasture. Thereafter, morning and evening, as cooler temperatures prevailed, I wheeled loads of firewood up the path to the woodshed and stacked them inside with a smug satisfaction that grew as steadily as the neat rows themselves. The roosters, after initial clucks of alarm, quickly overcame their trepidation around the strangeness of a wheelbarrow once they discovered the bug-infested beauty of firewood stored on damp ground. Each piece I lifted was immediately eclipsed by two eager heads with enormous red combs twitching excitedly as they minutely scanned all sides of the wood, picking off bugs and slugs. Then I'd be trailed up the path to the woodshed where, after unloading my cargo (much lightened by the lack of bugs!), I would tip out the bits of bark and other debris for 'the boys' to scratch through—just in case we'd missed any wriggles. Finally, we'd all head back to the woodpile where once again, each piece was thoroughly examined and debugged before being loaded. I may have stacked wood more quickly in previous years, but I certainly had more entertainment with Bubble and Squeak 'helping.'

Their delight in bugs was equally matched by a delicious new thrill—raspberries. The small patch which borders my path was quickly picked clean along the edges. Then, whenever

I clambered through the tangled thorny canes filling my bucket, two pairs of eyes would follow my every move. As I gathered a few in my hand, I'd look out over the shoulder-high foliage and raise my arm: two heads would shoot up in expectation and I'd toss the berries towards them. I doubt if they ever hit the ground.

The preceding autumn I'd been lucky enough to pick a bumper crop of foxberries, which had also become a favourite with the boys. Though Bubble and Squeak were only two to three months old at the time, they had gorged happily whilst I sat packing the rest for the freezer. Bubble, when he could eat no more, had stretched himself along the length of my arm on his side while I worked, his legs languidly drooping in front, his crop solid with foxberries, his eyes sleepy with repletion.

The boys were also willing 'helpers' with the produce I grew for us all in raised beds on a southern slope. They never invaded the garden but would watch eagerly from the path as I moved among the plants filling my basket. Offerings of cucumbers or tomatoes seldom failed to come their way.

Another project on my list was the disintegrating deck at the rear of the house. Having already crashed through it suddenly while in the throes of carving a sculpture, I'd resigned myself to the work of replacing it and ordered the necessary lumber. The roosters, however, soon taught me to consider the ensuing upheaval as fun, not drudgery. As I cleared out the old wood, they quickly moved in and scratched happily through the damp, exposed earth. Bugs of all descriptions scurried amongst their busy toes while exuberant clucks rang out as special favourites were caught and devoured. I took tea breaks with Bubble and Squeak on my knees and sawed each board with a rooster balanced on the other end.

Twice they let out low clucks of alarm behind me, as though feeling somewhat endangered. The first time I looked round, a plump porcupine was waddling past, peering about shortsightedly but secure in his armour of rustling quills. The second alarm was the sighting of a cat creeping towards the birdfeeding stations, and I drove it away with rousing threats.

The skunk lurking under the shrubbery beside the stacked lumber I discovered for myself.

MEANWHILE, a daily gathering of varied insects was still necessary for Puck and I began to worry about his winter nutrition. He was the only bird of my acquaintance who absolutely disliked mealworms—my usual mainstay for feeding songbirds through the winter. Nor, for that matter, did he like cheese, tofu, raisins, bread, pasta or fresh fruits— proven avian favourites. Not even chokecherries.

Moths were a favourite, but their quantities were dwindling in the cooler weather and would be nonexistent in winter. Field insects gathered by sweeping the meadows with a large cloth bag were acceptable, but his fussy palate chose only certain ones and ignored the majority. His real joy seemed to be landing on the bug bag and riding on it out to the screened porch where I emptied it. He also loved prying open fresh cabbage heads for hidden worms or rooting through ears of corn seeking large, juicy borers. One friend, arriving with offerings of vegetables from her own garden, held open her bag only to stand astonished as Puck landed first on her hand, then jumped down into the bag when he spotted the corn. Unfortunately, these delicacies favoured by Puck had a very limited season. Even catching grasshoppers in mid-hop and flies in mid-zoom seemed more of a game than a desire for food.

He often sampled my own meals but usually dropped each morsel with every indication of disgust, wiped his beak and flew off. Human fare of which he wholeheartedly approved included de-alcoholized beer, corn chips (the rustle of the bag would bring him instantly) and a tofu cheese-substitute, provided it was offered in morsels on my tongue—tidbits left out for him would be ignored. Banking on his curiosity about wrapped food and his skill in puncturing packages, I left wrapped tofu cheese on the counter in the hopes that he'd have more appetite for food that he could 'sneak'—but to no avail. I usually wedged an apple each day into the crossbars of the easel for the roosters to eat and Puck, too, would share a little. Overall, his dislikes outweighed his likes and I became very concerned about his winter diet.

I finally brought in a colony of delightful European brown crickets to live among the bricks under the woodstove. Hopefully, they'd provide another source of nutrition but Puck turned up his beak at them and I consoled myself with the joys of crickets singing throughout the snowy months. Wanderers from the brick stronghold were eagerly snapped up by the less fastidious roosters.

At length, as the brisk fall days merged into winter and outside insects were no longer available, Puck compromised about the mealworms: he'd eat them, but *only* the pupae—which, of course, were the least plentiful.

However, Puck always loved games with foods he didn't particularly care to eat, and mere words are inadequate to describe the feeling of dropped blueberries rolling down under one's shirt, or settling in one's bra. The squirmy sensation of an unsuspecting bare foot descending in the night on a damp chanterelle mushroom discarded by Puck was also unforgettable. One day, an unusual clink on the oven racks of the electric stove revealed a dry curled appleskin with a cargo of two fat mealworms which Puck had been carrying in his bill earlier. It had evidently been dropped through a (fortunately) cold burner and had gradually worked down to the oven. I reflected gratefully that I'd had no occasion to switch on the oven for supper. Over the years, I have found mealworms in the woodbox, in the bathroom, in my bed, in the power box, in my shoes, and even in my paintwater—but I would never have suspected their presence in the oven.

Puck and the roosters working together could initiate a real power play in the kitchen. One hurried suppertime, when I was due to leave the house immediately after eating, found Puck sitting on a heating saucepan flicking out uncooked pasta shells to Bubble and Squeak circling below while I hastily chopped onions nearby. Another day, a paint-sodden paper towel protruded from my shirt pocket while I wrapped leftovers from supper. Bubble was nibbling persistently at my toes, his particular signal for wanting a treat, and Puck was darting energetically at the plastic wrap trying to puncture it. As I finally opened the fridge door, Puck jerked out the paper towel and dropped it on the floor. With clucks of joy, the roosters hurled themselves on it while I simultaneously stepped on it to prevent paint getting into their mouths. It all happened in an instant—just long enough for Puck to triumphantly pierce the package in my hand.

WHEN THE temperatures no longer rose above 5°C and occasional snowflurries whitened the land, the roosters were again confined to the house until spring. Squeak's plumage, though beautiful, was still inadequate for cold exposure and a busy winter of avian activities was interwoven with my own.

Each morning I rose at dawn to the joyous crowing of Bubble and Squeak from the studio. Like all birds, they greeted every day as though *this* were the one for which they'd been waiting. I kindled the fire and stepped outside to stock the birdfeeders, bang the ice out of the waterdish and fill it at the outside tap until the tap was eventually lost under mounting drifts of snow. Then I topped up the woodbox, took a brief walk before returning to a warmed house, ate breakfast and carried my coffee over to the armchair.

At this point, the roosters would be waiting tensely on the other side of the studio door for the Great Morning Rooster Romp. I'd stroll casually towards their door, humming nonchalantly and unhook it. Then I'd race at top speed through the dining room and kitchen back to my chair, two wildly-excited roosters thudding behind in hot pursuit. If I wasn't fast enough, Bubble would nip my heels but if I got safely to home base, I'd spin around, crouch, and he'd leap into my arms for an ecstatic hug.

Try as he would, Squeak was seldom ahead of Bubble. Excitement over, we'd all cuddle down in the chair while I read, finished my beverage and wondered vaguely how less eccentric people started each day.

The roosters, like other birds, also had their devilish sides and certain days found them more than usually persistent at pulling books out of bookcases, lunging at my feet to nip my toes or 'pruning' houseplants. Sometimes they'd cooperate in certain nefarious plots with exasperating skill—as when Squeak stood guard with his beady eyes watching me in feigned innocence while, just out of my range of vision, Bubble quietly hacked away at a cherished Christmas cactus. Another day found them taking full advantage of my intense preoccupation with creating a clay sculpture to pull out a looseleaf binder packed with recipes and scratch the entire collection into shreds.

Even the other birds could fall victim to their mischievous impulses. One quiet evening in the living room saw both roosters dozing contentedly in my lap and Puck asleep on my shoulder. After an hour or so, I needed to get a book from the studio at the other end of the house. I coaxed the disgruntled, protesting roosters off my lap and walked away, Puck still on my shoulder. At this moment, I chanced to look back and catch Bubble's eyes gleaming devilishly as he leaped for my feet. With a squeal, I bolted forward, completely dislodging Puck, galloped through the unlit dining room and jerked wide the half-open door, Bubble hard on my heels. Molly, sound asleep on top of the door, suddenly found herself in mid-air and flapped wildly. This shot her abruptly into the darkened studio where she careened into Desmond dozing on a shelf. Desmond, finding himself suddenly attacked in the night, stoutly retaliated, and the two pigeons fought fiercely with sharp coos and flailing wings. Bubble, meanwhile, succeeded in tripping me into the easel while Squeak, abandoned in the living room and hearing bewildering bedlam erupt in the studio, broke into shrill clucking at the top of his lungs.

I sensed that the upcoming winter could be an interesting one.

CHAPTER EIGHT

A Busy Winter

I REMEMBER A FRIEND MANY YEARS AGO, upon hearing that I was moving to the country, asking in all seriousness, "But what will you do during those long winter evenings?"

Of all possible answers, I never thought that indoor bird-watching would be the most likely reply.

The 'long winter evenings' were definitely a high point of each day for the roosters since we usually spent those times together in a companionable heap in my armchair—a relaxing close to a day of intense studio work. As soon as I sat down with my feet on the ottoman, Bubble would leap onto my legs while Squeak would take over my lap. Occasionally, in their eagerness, they'd leap up from either side simultaneously only to collide with one another and slide back to the floor in a splutter of annoyed clucks. Eventually we'd all be settled and cozy for the next few hours, the roosters basking and blissful as I slowly stroked their backs or ran my fingers through their beautiful, curved 'sickle' feathers. Bubble's eyes would be nearly closed in rapture except for a tiny twinkle of light as he sat across my legs watching my face; but when I met his gaze, the twinkle would slowly be extinguished as he sank into sleep, snoring lightly. Eventually, he'd pick his way around Squeak's recumbent form and stand close to my face for a luxurious hour of concentrated cuddling—at times, in his delight, drooling shamelessly.

Squeak, too, adored being stroked over and over and would lie first one way, then another, and most often with his tail feathers against my front so that his back would receive the full benefit of my attentions. Two or three times he'd feel the need to stand up suddenly and 'reset' his plumage with a vigorous shake before resuming his place. If he flapped his wings as well, swelling out with an obvious desire to crow, I'd tell him firmly, pointing for emphasis, to get down, go around the corner and use his 'crowing stool' if he felt that way—that laps were for quiet roosters only. His knowing eye would indicate quite clearly that he understood, even if he didn't agree, and usually he lay back down quietly. Otherwise, he'd stalk unwillingly off to his stool, perhaps loosing a single, piercing crow en route, his head turned to check my reaction.

All too soon, it seemed to the roosters, I'd be coaxing them off my lap and flexing my legs to see if they were still operable. Then I'd bed the boys down for the night in the studio, a timely sprinkle of shelled sunflower seeds or shredded cocunut countering their good-natured grumblings. Should evening visitors prevent our usual cuddle time, Bubble would often lie just inside the studio door obviously waiting for them to go and leaping up hopefully, not to mention tactlessly, any time I passed the door.

Multi-natured Puck would doze each evening inside my shirt, peering up at me with bright, tiny eyes, his feathers fluffed out in repose and trustfulness—or he'd pop out fiendishly to pry through Squeak's plumage (who'd ignore him)—or to pull Bubble's tail feathers (anathema to Bubble's innate dignity) and he'd rise in annoyance and whisk them away. Puck's mischievous character also delighted in his 'cuckoo act' when he'd pop his head out of my shirt from between buttons, nip my fingers and as quickly pop back in, all in a split-second flash that was beyond my sluggish efforts to retaliate by grabbing his beak—one of our favourite games.

Another ploy for teasing me was for Puck to rustle my hair in the vicinity of my ear as though he were about to thrust his bill inside, his head cocked for any reaction, his crest feathers up. I'd eye him sideways threateningly, while he gazed up with twinkling eyes, the picture of innocence. When I resumed my reading or my thoughts, he'd wait a moment, then gently pry the hair aside again over my ear while my every nerve tingled in horrendous anticipation. I'd resolutely ignore him, muttering dire threats but would never know if he'd stop at that point, or would suddenly jam his beak well into my ear and dart away, ecstatic devilishness emanating like a comet's tail behind him while I writhed and howled.

It could be an amusing game—if one were the starling.

Puck's jealousy could be quite explicit. Whenever I sat next to the one-way glass overlooking the dining room feeder, thrilling to ultra-close observations of wild birds, he'd land on my head and slide slowly but compellingly down my hair in front of my face until I finally put up a finger perch. Then he'd bounce down onto it and stand facing me, trying to intercept my gaze, shifting his position as necessary to emphasize his own presence and hopefully cut off my view of anyone else. I could rarely resist peering around him insistently or pretending not to see him at all. I had so few opportunities for a little revengeful teasing.

Sunbathing was pure delight for Puck, as for any birds I've known, and he'd sprawl perfectly motionlessly in the radiant warmth, every feather lifted as the heat seeped under, his eyes glazed and unblinking, his open beak drinking in the sunshine. On gloomy days, when his desire for a sun bath would prove overwhelming, he'd climb down inside a crocheted lampshade on a hanging lamp and bask on the inner rim with gloriously-spread wings next to a sixty-watt bulb. Whenever I opened the front doors of the woodstove, drew up my chair and toasted my toes, Puck would scamper down my legs to my feet. There he'd hold out his wings in the heat rather like a cormorant, his head bristling to twice its normal size as all his feathers stood on end, his mouth opened wide to drink in the glory. Other days he'd perch on the metal guard shielding the rear of the woodstove and absorb constant delicious warmth in defiance of winter's inexorable grip.

His plumage by this point was fully adult, the dusky juvenile colouring having given way to glorious iridescent glossiness studded with stars—from which starlings gain their name. His tiny eyes twinkled continually like two more stars, his beak was sunshine yellow and his legs looked dark but had an unusual reddish glow. I'd find myself visually pondering this tantalizing 'Milky Way' plumage, and ideas of rendering Puck's starry plumage in cosmic terms gradually began to coalesce.

One afternoon while I was busy in the kitchen I heard Puck repeating the strangest sound as he amused himself on the electric stove, reaching for charred tidbits under the cold burners. It sounded like 'e-e-e-e-aw-w-w' and had a peculiar, plaintive ring. His behaviour seemed normal and he wasn't ailing or injured but I couldn't decipher the message at all—till I entered the bath-room. As I opened the door, the antique hinges protested loudly with an 'e-e-e-e-aw-w-w'! Puck, in true starling fashion, was becoming a mimic.

He soon began 'taping' other sounds which he frequently noticed, including a strange, nasal 'bang-bang' which I never did identify. The pièce de résistance came one day when he was perched by a studio window chattering and singing. Suddenly, in perfectly recognizable English, he said "Tut! tut! tut!... you're such a precious little bird."

I felt a rising glow of rosy embarrassment at the horror of other private 'sweet nothings,' destined only for the ears of my birds, becoming public knowledge.

As the winter season wore on, the drifts rose higher and high-er and my oft-shovelled path to the road soon resembled a tun-nel. Snow weighed down the spruce branches, forming so many safe hidey-holes in the trees that shy Ruffed Grouse would roost overnight right beside the house. As the outside doors all opened outwards, emerging from the house some mornings presented a formidable challenge. The snow-laden skylight and encrusted north windows dimmed the usual brightness in the studio and many times the kitchen window was completely plastered with snow from the north wind. I'd reach a broom out over the huge mound of snow banked against the kitchen wall and brush off the glass and thermometer, although windy days would usually coat them again.

One afternoon, light-hearted confusion reigned indoors,

contrasting sharply with the silent winter beauty outside. I had bottled one batch of home brew and set another to ferment while the clutter of bottles everywhere suggested an unusual rakish rowdiness that was difficult to ignore. I'd also re-potted a large but ailing houseplant on the floor, trying in vain to confine the dirt to strategically-placed newspapers. Puck, however, had discovered a flourishing colony of tiny grubs among the roots and in a wild digging frenzy had gobbled down the lot. He had also spent a glorious half-hour prying up pictures and mirrors on the wall to let them bang down again over and over so that now they all hung askew. The roosters, frisky and devilish, engaged each other in mock cockfights, hooked magazines off the table, scratched through the potting soil when my attention was elsewhere, chased my feet and contributed generously in other ways to the general mayhem. Molly had claimed the upstairs as her own private territory and each time Desmond emerged into view, she'd swoop down the stairwell and, with flailing wings, drive him back to the studio. Then, satisfied, she'd soar through the kitchen to the upstairs again—till Desmond made another attempt to join the rest of the family.

In the midst of all this, I'd had word of a sale of artwork (received with Puck balancing dexterously on the extended telephone cord), had swung Bubble around and around the livingroom in celebration and had just scooped Squeak up into my arms in the kitchen. Suddenly I paused, Puck landing at that moment on my head, as I sensed an alien thread in our conviviality. I turned with a start to the kitchen window.

There, kneeling on top of the snow, directly in front of the small square window, were two neighbourhood children muffled in snowsuits against the cold. Each child had her thumb comfortably in her mouth and each, with revolving eyes of wonder, was as mesmerized by my private life as by a favourite television show.

I could only hope that their parents wouldn't believe them.

THE ARTWORK, despite avian 'assistance,' flourished throughout the winter months as the light pouring through the cleared skylight lingered a little longer each day.

Squeak still tugged my pant leg for attention while I painted, and loved sitting in my lap during working hours or, on rare occasions, balancing precariously on my shoulder, where his weight seemed suddenly doubled. Both roosters still continued to steal and shred my paper towels and, to my surprise and dismay, Desmond too began shredding the roll I stored above high chicken-tide level. Together he and Puck would worry it till it finally tumbled to the waiting beaks circling below. If I were not home to interfere, Bubble and Squeak would unwind and shred the entire roll over the length of the studio floor.

Puck concentrated on chasing my moving brush either from the top of the canvas or by landing directly on my hand. Should I foil him too skilfully each time, he'd try dabbling in jars of paint water, which he knew perfectly well was forbidden, and I was driven, for his own safety, to contrive a wooden casing over them. Pieces of chalk or expensive willow charcoal were often whisked away, sometimes right out of my hand, rarely to be seen again—or worse, to be crunched accidentally underfoot later. A newly-inked linoprint was jerked cleanly out of my grasp and dropped halfway across the studio just as I'd eased it gently off the wet block. Even Molly contributed her share as seeds rolled from her shelf above the easel and lodged themselves inside the paintings between canvas and backing. Unknown to the general viewing public, many of my artworks rattle when shaken.

Acrylic paintings must be laid flat for varnishing, a highly vulnerable position in such a lively household. The process, therefore, is fraught with anxiety, despite the advantage of rapid drying, and waving the wet brush wildly in wordless threats has never been recommended in the directions on the label. Even so, I have found it imperative to stand guard over each piece until it is completely dry and can be covered by a cloth. Most crises over the years have occurred just as I turned my back to put the brush

Squeak reclining on the couch (top).

Chip the grackle on Squeak's back (above).

Puck, the baby starling, who arrived with the nickname 'Jaws' (above).

Puck bathing in the roosters' water dish (left).

Puck in her personal hidey-hole. Her dusky juvenile head contrasts sharply with her starry adult body (right).

Puck, with tufts of baby down, inside my shirt (below).

Squeak 'helping' with the firewood.

Puck sunning on my hand (above).

Puck sunning in a euphoric trance (right).

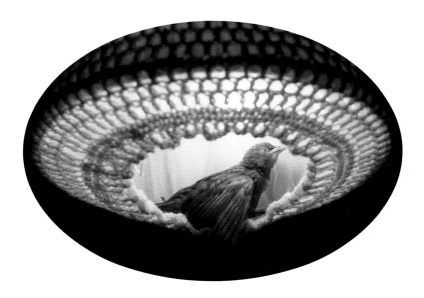

Puck enjoying a heat bath inside a lamp (above).

Puck's starry adult plumage is just beginning to emerge (left).

Puck's famous toilet roll spin (right).

Puck inside a clay sculpture, following her nest-building instinct (below).

Cresting the Starry Way, *acrylic on paper, takes inspiration from Puck as she streaks onward and upward in a blaze of stars, carrying our life essence to crest despite clutching pitfalls (above).*

Puck's full adult plumage inspired Cresting the Starry Way *(left).*

into water, but with an ever-developing ability to reverse emergencies, the damage isn't discernable by the time the canvas is ready for a show.

The paintings were usually protected from the inevitable droppings by sheets, and those projectiles which found their mark were cleaned off fairly easily. One day I hauled out a painting which had been started and abandoned some months previously. I had neglected to cover it and a liberal streaking of droppings oozing down the surface encrusted one end. The piece, although stored on its longer edge, was vertical in format and as I stood it upright on the easel, the elongated blobs floated horizontally in an underwater area that had been destined to show fish. I eyed the placing of the droppings critically. Without a doubt, their random patterning was far superior to anything I could produce and with renewed interest I carefully outlined each dropping with a fish-like line. When the paint was dry, I scrubbed the canvas clean of faeces and painted the fish in whole. Then I successfully completed the painting. Those in the know agreed wholeheartedly that Puck's name should really be signed beside mine on *The Eternal Flow*—an apt title.

At this juncture, I had to retrieve a showing of artworks from Halifax. This involved scheduling a time convenient to everyone involved, as well as allowing for at least five hours of highway travel. The morning I was due to leave, Puck flew out from his nightime roost among the stored canvases in the studio with the entire top of his head above the eyes completely denuded of feathers. The skin looked inflamed and red, and he scratched repeatedly at it. Horrified, I postponed the trip for that day and as soon as office hours permitted, telephoned the vet. Then I drove hastily to town for a soothing, antiseptic ointment which I applied daily to the skin for the next few days. With the first application, Puck ceased scratching and the skin gradually resumed its normal colouring. The feathers, too, grew in eventually but I never did fathom the cause of Puck's mysterious baldness. Whether they believed me or not, those in charge of the

Halifax gallery certainly acknowledged that my excuse for pro-
longing the exhibit by one day was original.

Another of my winter projects was to produce *Spiritus*, a
second book of linoprints and poems expressing our inner journey in images inspired by many birds I've known. As in an earlier book, I was again designing and laying out each page myself to
save costs. This simple-sounding phrase signified the big studio
table being snowed under layers of acetate sheets, P.M.T. copies
of linoprints, endless pages of text and page numbers and an
increasing clutter of clippings. A massive paper cutter, razor-
sharp, dominated one end and ever-elusive gluesticks and scissors
hid themselves with ease everywhere. Puck gloried in the confusion, stole carefully trimmed words straight out of my fingers, ate
glue to an extent that would have been lethal for anyone else and
threatened me with heart failure by making lightning darts for
pieces of paper just as the guillotine blade on the cutter
whumped down with a screeching thud.

There were moments when I wondered weakly if either of us
would live long enough to see the book completed.

The medium of clay sculpture proved to be as engrossing for
Puck as for me but at least I had the unusual satisfaction of
knowing that none of the wet clay in his mouth would harm
him. He'd climb all over each piece as I formed it, stippling the
surface by repeatedly poking his beak into the clay and prying it
open. Small lumps began to appear all over the house and I had
quite an accumulation in my hair and on my shoulders from
Puck fastidiously wiping his beak on me. When each sculpture
reached the leather-hard stage I'd try, often fruitlessly, to hide it
from him since punctures at that point involved fussy repairs,
and his abrupt landings on drying projecting parts could snap
them off.

At this time, when late winter began reluctantly to yield to
spring's persuasive powers, I discovered that Puck, unbelievably, was a female! I gazed at her in astonishment, utterly
unable to picture her as a gentle, nurturing mother bird but

the big reference book I had consulted was adamant: the iris of female starlings was pale, as was Puck's; the base of the bill pinkish or buffy, as was Puck's. As though in confirmation, Puck began exploring all starling-sized cavities around her with a new seriousness that hinted at possible nesting aspirations, and one of the first that caught her fancy was a recumbent clay sculpture. Each finished work at the leathery stage had been cut into sections, hollowed and reassembled. This one I had laid on its side in order to smooth the bottom and incise the title. Puck, perhaps with spring urging her on, bustled imperiously past me and climbed inside, chattering excitedly to herself and examining every hump and hollow to the very end.

Many have been the comments engendered by my clay sculptures but no one, to that date, had ever suggested raising a family inside them.

As Puck's spring energies continued to rise like the renewing sap in trees, she began wild flights indoors over and over as though migrating—similar to robin friends in earlier years. Most starlings do migrate although some winter in nearby cities where enough food can be scrounged. A few have frequented my feeding stations but for the suet, not the seeds. Puck's wild flighting hour after hour was so compulsive and tiring that she'd stumble clumsily whenever she stopped and during one such landing skidded off my head and tumbled straight into a frying pan of scrambled eggs I was stirring.

Her capacity for teasing also increased and Desmond, lying in privacy under the studio lounge chair with its protective blanket draped around him, would discover Puck poking her beak through the blanket at him. Ever guarding his territorial rights, Desmond would retaliate and the two of them would batter vigorously at one another through the folds. Her mania for rooting through potted plants also accelerated during this period with the scented geranium being the only one to respond to such treatment with enthusiasm. For the first time, it actually bloomed.

Puck's persistent explorations of cupboards, small boxes, purses and anything else that even remotely suggested a tree hole led me to contrive special 'treehouses' for her out of wood or cardboard, with starling-sized apertures and a handful of dried grass inside. She examined them all with zeal but without commitment, preferring instead to drag beakloads of long grasses in among my stored paintings. There, on top of some early landscapes, she concocted a very loosely-assembled mess that could only be described as a nest by a most ardent ornithologist.

Puck's fussiness with food at last abated somewhat and she deigned to eat mealworms so avidly that my colony was soon seriously depleted. I decided to get a new supply the day I was scheduled to have repairs done to the van and drove to town on one of the dreariest of March days. Dirty snow and slush still sloshed underfoot, making walking treacherous, and intermittent drizzle with a piercing wind added the final touch. I left the van at the garage and returned an hour later, a big jar of mealworms held next to me under my coat. Due to unforeseen difficulties, the work was going to take longer than I had anticipated but I still had several errands. I could manage them on foot.

The mealworms, however, presented a problem and I eyed the garage proprietor speculatively.

"I wonder if I might ask you a favour."

"Well, sure you can," he bellowed pleasantly.

"It's rather odd, I'm afraid."

"Oh no, I'm sure it's okay." Courtesy was his motto.

"You see, I have birds at home and I have here a jar of mealworms for them. It's too cold outside to carry them about. Do you mind if I leave them in your office till the van is ready?"

He was visibly startled. "A jar of what?"

"Mealworms. See?" I held them up briefly, followed by his bulging eyes. "They can't get out. It's just that they mustn't get cold." I wrapped the jar warmly in my scarf and placed it gently on his desk. He watched me like one in a trance.

"Worms?"

"Yes."

His face was a study in mystification. "A jar of worms?" he reiterated, trying to get this straight.

"Yes. They need to keep warm."

He puckered his brow. "What did you say they were for?"

"My birds. I have birds that need insects in the winter and I get these from a friend at the university."

"Oh-h-h, the university," he agreed, as though that explained everything. I wondered in what fascinating ways the university had earned the eccentric reputation which obviously flourished in his mind. He spoke as one who has seen it all. He stood staring into space a moment, then focused aburptly on the bundle on his desk. "Let's see them again."

I unwrapped the jar and held it up once more. "See? They can't get out, they're quiet and not vicious. They won't be a mite of trouble."

This effort at humour passed unnoticed. He peered closely at them.

"Worms ..." he murmured, looking at me thoughtfully.

"I feed them to my birds." I wanted to get clear just who was intending to eat them.

"Y-e-s ..." he mused. "So you have birds."

I felt we were getting somewhere. "Yes."

"That's different."

"I suppose so."

"What kind of birds?"

I had been waiting for this and was determined to spare myself unnecessary embarrassment by suppressing any mention of roosters.

"Starlings."

"Starlings?" in disbelief. I nodded. He grunted disparagingly.

"They're very interesting," I countered defensively.

"I suppose so." Never argue with a customer. He reflected awhile longer. "Well ... some people have cats and some have dogs ..."

I agreed. "And I have birds."

"Ye-e-s. Do you have cages full of them?"

I shuddered at the image. "No," I said firmly, "they have the run of the house."

A mistake. His eyes widened and I could see the inevitable conclusion forming in his mind about foot-deep droppings carpeting the floors.

"How many do you have?" he gasped.

I mentally transposed the roosters into starlings and added the result. "Three" I replied; then added quickly, "They're really fun to know. So I'll just leave the worms here, okay?"

"Oh sure. That's fine ... birds, eh? Well, that's real interesting. I don't know that I'd pick starlings though ..."

"Well, sometimes they pick you. You take in a stranded nestling but when you try to release it, it won't leave. Then one things leads to another ..."

"M-m-m, yes, I see ... well now," he said briskly, "You learn something new every day."

I fled before he could change his mind.

Two hours later, I returned to the garage laden with full shopping bags and set them down thankfully. Then I tucked the mealworms into my purse and sank into a chair. Soon a young mechanic bustled in to tell me the van was ready. I settled my bill, loaded the groceries and began backing carefully out of the garage into a noisy congestion of people and vehicles. The proprietor was busily tinkering with the underside of a car on the hoist. Suddenly he appeared in the doorway.

"HEY!" he bellowed.

All heads instantly turned, no doubt wondering if I were trying to leave without paying. In an ear-splitting voice easily capable of lifting Puck straight off her perch at home, he roared, to everyone's astonishment, "DIDJA GET YER WORMS?"

Months later at the same garage, a new gas tank had been ordered for me and I'd left my phone number so I could be notified the moment it arrived. A few days passed while I kept a pan under the dripping van and wondered restlessly what on earth was causing the delay. Then I got a phone call, not from the garage, but from a friend.

"You're not by any chance waiting for a gas tank?"

"How did you know?" I asked, mystified. The 'bush telegraph' in our small town has always amazed me, but this was ridiculous.

Evidently her mother was a customer of lifelong standing at the garage and when my name and phone number were accidentally discarded, the proprietor called her. He was aware that her daughter was the Animal Care Technician at the university. The woman in turn phoned her daughter to see if she knew of anyone who "drove a gray van and carried around jars of worms!"

As SPRING FINALLY ASSERTED ITSELF and the last snows wilted in the increasing warmth, I brought home feed bags heavy with horse manure and dug over the garden. Buds were sticky on the trees, spring migrants were hailed each day with delight and I gathered enough fiddleheads to freeze for winter. Puck amused herself with uncurling the fronds but preferred to eat them steamed and buttered.

I also began leaving the outside porch door ajar in the evenings in order to lure moths inside for Puck to enjoy the following day. Instead, each evening, strange bumbling and twanging noises would reveal a huge porcupine ponderously climbing up inside the screens with his long claws for reasons obscure to the rest of us. I would remonstrate sternly with him through the glass door while Puck, clinging to the nape of my neck, peered around my head at him, her eyes wide with concern and her starry crest feathers erect with anxiety.

Late one morning, a woman arrived with a male Rosebreasted Grosbeak in a small box. He had struck her window at least half an hour earlier. Since he was still incapacitated, she was concerned for his well-being and left him with me.

I held the little visitor for a long while in my hands so that he could stabilize from the added shock of a car ride. Gradually, his tensions eased and I held a cup of water to his beak. He showed no interest until I dabbled my finger in it, stirring the water into ripples of light. Then I held a gleaming, tantalizing drop from the tip of my finger before his fascinated eyes and he touched his beak to it, swallowing it eagerly. After sipping another couple of drops from my finger, he finally lowered his head and drank deeply from the cup.

Puck landed on my head at that moment, spotted the visitor and bounced down onto my arm, an amusing conflict of curiosity and jealousy. She edged closer to the grosbeak. He eyed her mildly while she examined him minutely, her head feathers bristling. Satisfied at last, she lingered, preening, and I could see her evident trust in me dissolving the last of the grosbeak's trepidation at my presence. When Puck finally flitted off, the grosbeak flew into the porch and hung on the screening, beating his wings strongly and normally.

Moments later, he was soaring through the trees.

PUCK BEGAN these days to show a high interest in accompanying me outside to fill the feeders and to plant vegetable seeds, taking short flights around the trees with obvious enjoyment. I wondered bleakly if she would choose to leave—perhaps to fulfil her nesting aspirations.

The choice to stay or leave must always be left to a bird in excellent health and although Puck was certainly in good form, her indoor existence had had certain minor effects on her: her upper mandible during the winter had gradually protruded three-eighths of an inch beyond her lower one; a natural life in the wild, perhaps prodding harder materials all day in search of food, may have prevented this. Also, the base of her upper mandible had always remained mysteriously bare of feathers, something I'd never noticed in wild starlings. Finally, her legs appeared to have thickened slightly this spring and she'd bite at them as though they gave discomfort; perhaps constant landings over and over on window perches during her 'migration' were the cause and although I'd wrapped those surfaces with carpet underlay recently, they may have taken their toll. All other landing areas in the house had always been padded—a lesson learned from robin friends.

Then one beautiful morning as we planted lettuce seeds together, Puck seemed unusually high-strung, darting away and returning repeatedly. Suddenly she swooped around the corner of the house and I never saw her again.

When Puck had first come to me, seventeen months after I'd lost County the robin, with whom I'd shared the extraordinary experience of courtship and parenthood, I'd made every effort to continue my art. I still had many of County's teachings to express but, despite that, I couldn't work and sank into month after month of depression, grateful for the comforting companionship of the roosters and pigeons. But Puck's ongoing demanding personality had positively goaded me into continually responding with the result that, four months after her arrival, I was again working daily in the studio—'helped' by her persistent devilishness. When she flew out of my life, I had no sense of final loss or of her nearby presence in the natural world. She seemed to have slipped into another reality—as though her mission had been fulfilled.

She left exactly a year to the day, almost to the hour, that she'd arrived.

In *Cresting the Starry Way* (illustrated) Puck, studded with stars of illumination, streaks onward and upward with her characteristic drive and vitality, bearing my sluggish self as in a soulboat of safety above the sadness that had persisted in pulling me down. So, in a greater way, must we follow our inner guides to crest after crest of challenge despite the doubts and other pitfalls that clutch at us from below like claws.

CHAPTER NINE

More Avian Adventures

Two days after Puck's departure, a friend brought me a tiny female Purple Finch who had been noticed in a poor condition at someone's feeder. She was very weak but her eyes were bright and knowing—a good sign. She showed no sign of internal injury and her beautiful plumage of woven earth colours was unmarred.

I turned a small box on its side, layered it inside with soft towels and set it at eye-level on a shelf. Then I placed a jar lid of water within, to which had been added avian vitamin powder and tetracycline. Beside it was another lid of wild bird seed mixed with budgie gravel. The little finch I laid gently on the towels inside the box.

From the beginning, 'Sweetie' fed herself without assistance and gradually gained enough mobility to hop slowly out of her box along the shelf and back. I began placing her dishes at the end of the shelf to stimulate further motivation. A few days later, when Squeak leaped up enthusiastically onto a bench just below her shelf, she was startled into a spontaneous flight of about two yards. In another two days, she was living in the screened porch, roosting each night on branches (nailed permanently near the rafters for just such occasions) and flighting down to her food and water on the table below.

One week to the day, Sweetie was flying so strongly that I was delighted to be able to restore her to outdoor freedom. She was one of the most charming of creatures, always twinkling cheerfully.

By this time, spring migrants were settling down everywhere, staking out territories and beginning nesting activities. Friends of mine, who were avid birdwatchers, had discovered a robin's nest being built deep in the woods about a mile from my house. Unfortunately, it was placed on top of a seven-foot tall tree trunk—the remains of a spruce tree which had been snapped off leaving a splintered ring perfectly formed to hold a nest in place. We were all concerned that lack of camouflage would leave the eggs and nestlings vulnerable to raids by hawks, crows or jays. Perhaps too the mother, brooding so openly, would fall victim at night to a hunting owl.

A special part of my heart is given over to robins and the next morning I set out to find the nest, carrying stout twine and a pocket knife. When I arrived, neither of the pair were at hand and I reached up and felt the damp inside cup of the nest. It was beautifully formed of mud and twigs and I realized that the robins were probably busy gathering soft materials for the lining on which the eggs would rest. Quickly I set to work in order to be gone when they returned.

I tied a cord around the trunk below the nest to form two loose loops. Then I thrust several live spruce boughs tightly under the cord so that their tops rose into arching greenery up and over the nest, hiding it from marauding eyes. I left a slight break in the foliage so that the returning female could indeed find her nest, and sped twenty feet away to crouch down, hidden and still, my scope trained on the nest.

When the female arrived with a huge beakful of dried grass, she was visibly taken aback at the drastic landscaping done to the nest site in her absence. I smiled broadly as, in obvious perplexity, she hopped from tree to tree around the stump, eyeing it from every angle. Finally she landed on the spruce branches themselves, peering between them this way and that before dropping her grasses on top and flying off. I hoped that I hadn't shattered her confidence about using the nest, but three days later, I peered through the scope to see, amid the spruce greenery shielding the nest, a bright eye in a white eyering watching me warily.

Thereafter, I checked the situation regularly and one day noticed that the branches seemed to have slipped somewhat askew. Luck was with me since at that moment both parents were again temporarily absent. I ran to the nest, hurriedly jammed in a couple of extra branches but paused long enough to reach into the nest and thrill to the touch of four warm eggs. At that moment, barks of alarm suddenly broke out as both parents returned, outraged at my intrusion, and I fled before their verbal onslaught. Forty feet away, I stopped, turned my scope upon the nest and watched in delight as the female stepped in beside her eggs. In due time, the babies left the shelter of their nest to be taught the elements of survival by their father while their mother built a new nest elsewhere for her second clutch.

It was a privilege to have helped them with their first.

OVER THE YEARS, I have been lucky enough to have helped many juvenile or adult birds and each encounter has been unique and full of learning for me. As I sat wondering what the next adventure would be, I reflected on many who had gone before and their influence on my art.

A trio of hungry, week-old juncos were brought to me one summer's day, orphaned by one of those inexcusable dirt bikes that tear ruthlessly through natural habitat as though it were devoid of life. The parent bird had been crushed and one of the babies was found trying to hide under its dead wing. Hopefully, the entire clutch was rescued but one can't be sure.

The babies thrived though, as endearing a group as I've ever known. They very quickly gained confidence with me and enjoyed the freedom of the house, but tended to centre their activities around the 'bug box,' water dish, and indoor garden in the living room. Friends invited to supper preferred to stay with plates balanced precariously in their laps near the babies rather than sit with more ease in the dining room. The fluffy charm of the fledglings, their incredibly tiny toes and ridiculous stumpy bottoms had an irresistible attraction for all who saw them.

At first, they slept on towels in a warm, covered box but within days were roosting in the plants all night like small exotic flowerbuds. Daylight would find them sunning on windowsills, playing chase through the garden, learning to catch 'wrigglies' in the bug box and splashing happily in the waterdish. They enjoyed my company too, and one humorous moment found me grasping a mixing bowl with one hand and stirring muffin batter with the other, a junco perched on each wrist.

The dark side of caring for baby birds, as I have already noted, is the endless effort spent hunting for bugs and digging for worms. Substitutes like ground beef and canned cat and dog foods cannot supply adequate nutrition and can cause health problems from deficiency. Thus, so crucial does each individual 'wriggly' become in one's eyes that one can't afford to pass up any possible contributions.

As I re-entered the house one day with a scrambling selection in my container, I spotted an enormous spider against the hall ceiling. I was hot and tired, being dressed in smothery clothes for protection against mosquitoes and black flies. Rather than go back out and lug in the stepladder from the shed, I picked up a ruler in one hand and held the container up as high as I could stretch. Then I cautiously prodded the huge creature with the ruler, expecting him to fall in with the rest of the bugs.

Instead, he dropped into my sleeve.

With a howl, I dropped the container and leaped about in a frenzy, tearing frantically at my buttons and shaking my sleeve madly. The liberated bugs meanwhile, swarmed in all directions while I squealed and writhed, dancing among them like a demented dervish.

Dinner for the juncos was late that day.

When they could care for themselves completely, I released the youngsters into the birdfeeding area near the back door. Juncos were prominent among my regular 'clients' so the babes would easily find role models to complete their education. Regretfully, as usual, I watched them from the deck until they finally merged into the forest life around them. A couple of hours later, I discovered one hunting for bugs in all innocence out on the dirt road and carried him back to the feeding area. Already, he was indicating obvious trepidation towards me as a human— which was good to see.

Successive sightings of juvenile juncos near the house that summer always made me pause ... and wonder ...

ONE SUMMER, I had about six or seven baby sparrows and warblers simultaneously and all required feedings every twenty to thirty minutes. I also had a full schedule of my own concerns, so I would take them with me if there was any danger of being away from home too long.

During one busy excursion, a companion and I shared several stops in town, stopping as needed to feed the ever-hungry chorus in the back seat. When we pulled in at the feedstore, I busied myself inside with a lengthy list while my friend slipped into the back seat to feed the babies.

Deeply engrossed in her difficult job, she began to notice that the light was getting dimmer. One needs lots of light to push food into the back of a wriggling nestling's throat instead of into its eyes.

She glanced up. Surrounding the car was a silent cluster of grizzled, weatherbeaten farmers, their rapt faces crowding the windows, watching her every move with mystified fascination.

The irrepressible nature of nestlings, their paradoxical innocence and inherent wisdom, and the conflicting feelings I have releasing them into the remnants of the natural order have all borne fruit in the art work. Birds universally symbolize the spirit and I've placed nestlings in generative positions within compositions where their gaping poses, as seeking and needing nourishment, suggest the importance in our spiritual development of a receptive attitude when at the threshold of a new beginning, a new level of awareness.

Song of the Shell, *linoprint.*

In the print *Song of the Shell* (illustrated), an upright shell, generating energies and cradling nestlings, sings of eternal beginnings being released into the elements of air (with bird forms), earth (leaf forms), and water (fish) from the primal fire of creation.

ONCE, AN ORPHANED grackle arrived, a fluffy, eager-eyed youngster gaping hungrily. Adult grackles emit a distinctive 'chuck' sound and I began a habit of calling all grackles that I helped, 'Chuck.'

When he became old enough to feed himself, Chuck still pleaded to have the food pushed into his mouth by 'mom.' Instead, I'd set the dish resolutely in front of him, leave the room, and then peek warily. Chuck, ever hungry, would gape and cry persistently but when I failed to appear, he'd gaze at the food and gape at that instead. Then gradually he'd edge towards it and take a few tentative nibbles. But if he suddenly spotted me, he'd run towards me, gaping dramatically, like a little feathered charlatan.

Chuck loved sharing my dinners in the screened porch, but not everyone enjoyed his company. When a friend joined me one day for lunch, Chuck flew immediately onto her plate just as she sat down. Fearing the worst, she yelled and shooed him. Chuck, startled, shot a fluidy mess all over her dinner and flew to her beer glass. Outraged, she shrieked at what he had done, causing him promptly to do it again—this time, into her beer.

On another memorable day, the same much-tried friend was painting a poster in the living room when Chuck suddenly arrived on the scene. The two of them spotted the open bottle of ink at the same time—but Chuck got to it first. By the time I arrived in response to ear-splitting wails, there was ink all over the living room, Chuck was perched up as far out of reach as possible, the poster was ruined, and the friend sat huddled on the floor, streaked with tears and ink.

Chuck also joined me on a camping trip and his shadow flitting inside the lighted tent at night greatly entertained other campers nearby. He was one bird who never gained any distrust of other humans so that I never dared to release him, and he shared many an adventure over the years.

IN A FARMHOUSE kitchen one spring day was a box of peeping, scrambling ducklings and goslings—scrambling except for the lone gosling with the twisted leg who couldn't stand. He lay pushing his legs helplessly, but his yellow, downy head was held high and his eyes bright. I finally persuaded a reluctant, brusque farmer to let me take the lame gosling home.

But the rough manner hid gold.

"He'll need company," said the man gruffly, "Take the runt too," and he thrust the tiniest duckling into my hands beside the gosling.

'Tiny Tim' never managed to walk but he grew into a snowy, affectionate gander who would answer my hug by wrapping his long neck around mine. A young vet operated on Timmy's leg free of charge because he couldn't guarantee the result. When the cast was removed, Tim still couldn't stand. I made extensive efforts with a body sling but eventually gave up. Tim was fully grown and perhaps the walking muscles were unable by then to develop. But painfully clear in my memory is the radiant look in Tim's eyes when he chanced one day to push himself upright against an overturned canoe and took a few forward steps, sliding along the smooth support.

Timmy and 'Webs' (the duckling) were inseparable and Webs never strayed far from Timmy's 'goose caboose,' the hay-lined box which cradled him. Tim had a soft, high-pitched, breathy hiss that he used as a greeting to me and to Webs that was an excellent imitation of my habitual, drawn-out "hi-i-i-i-i, Tim." I was highly amused one day by his response when I set a tiny, baby rabbit before him. Intrigued by his visitor, Tim reached down his long graceful neck, peered into the little furry face and saluted him with "hi-i-i-i-i!"

When Tim was in high spirits, the fleshy knob at the base of his bill was quite firm, and his blue eyes bright and sparkling. But when he was depressed and needed a hug, the knob was wrinkled and soft, and his eyes dark and mournfully rounded. Like all birds, he was fastidious and although I freshened his bedding several times a day, some feathers were permanently soiled. I think that this, as well as his immobility, was terribly hard on his spirits. But he loved being snuggled down in my lap by the hour.

Tim planted in me a love of all geese and I've been immediately drawn to them whenever I see them. Once, sitting surrounded by resting Canada geese, becoming attuned to little waves of alarm or interest that rippled through the flock, I felt I was among friends. Whenever I hear them honking as they fly overhead, and whenever I use a goose image in work like *Bringing Back the Light*, where the passage of the flying goose transforms the darkness into light, I think of Tim's bright eyes and how glad I am that he finally flew free.

Webs was inconsolable at Tim's passing and would sit whimpering in my lap. At last I found her a duckling for company and called him 'Paddles' because of his ridiculous, but charming, big webs. Paddles grew into a handsome drake whereas Webs, who had abruptly stopped laying eggs when Tim died, now grew distinctive drake feathers and became a full drake for the rest of his/her life!

ONE OF THE MOST entrancing wild birds to stay temporarily with me was an adult Saw-whet Owl. He had been bumped by a car and was unable to fly. When he was delivered to me, wrapped in a blanket, he was rigid with fear and lay in my hands for more than an hour before suddenly standing up. From that point on, he was completely at ease, loved to have his head rubbed, ate readily from my fingers, and slept by day in hanging plants and in bookcases. He had a passion for drinking milk from an eyedropper (a recommendation from a book) and ate canned lean meat and cooked eggs mixed with cuttings from my hair for roughage.

One day, a neighbour stopped in with a freshly-killed mouse from a mousetrap—a present for 'Whoot.' No doubt she felt sympathy towards a carnivorous bird having to face convalescence with a vegetarian human. We placed the mouse before Whoot, who ignored it pointedly. Then we tied a string to the carcass and dragged it tantalizingly (we hoped) back and forth before him— while I quelled a rising nausea. His only response was to click his beak and shoot out one foot to stop the action. Then he looked away in complete disinterest.

The message was clear but I wasn't up to providing him with a live mouse.

When Whoot was ready to leave, he suddenly became very animated one night and made several restless flights about the house in the dark. Next evening at dusk, I took him outside. He sat quite still on my hand with only his head revolving as his golden eyes gloried in the familiar woodland world once more.

Indoors, his diminutive size had given him almost a toy-like effect but now, in his natural element, he had immense dignity. Suddenly, he lifted his wings and vanished into his world without a sound—an integral part of the night.

Whoot has surfaced several times in my artwork, usually guarding the threshold of a new awareness just as owls do, indeed, signify for us life within the mysterious world of darkness. They are also associated symbolically with dying and are natural choices as guardians of the soul's passage after death. In *The Doorwarden,* the tree of life, an upright, crenated shell, leafs out as the light of transfiguration glows alluringly inside and Whoot looms up on the threshold. The reddish colouring of the shell speaks of sacrifice and also full-blooded vitality, attributes of the tree of life.

HE WAS DELIVERED to the back door wrapped tightly in a blanket, his eyes listlessly following my movements, his breath coming in deep, laboured gasps—a juvenile Great Black-backed Gull too exhausted by sickness and malnutrition to struggle. He had been found wandering on a beach near a fishing village, unable to fly, too weak to swim, and unhappily providing amusement for a stray dog.

I laid him gently in a box in the studio, easing him out of the confines of the blanket as I did so. But he still drew each breath with desperate effort, his gaze now fixed despairingly on the floor, his head lowered and his whole body heaving. This was clearly not just a case of being overheated by a blanket so I hastily moved him outside, box and all. I had indoor birds to consider and contagion might be an issue. I examined his body for possible injuries but found only fleas. Still the heroic battle for one breath after another went on.

I carried his box to the truck and drove to the veterinary clinic, one hand gently caressing his neck feathers while I murmured soothingly to ease his fright. But he was too ill to struggle for freedom; the struggle for each breath was as much as he could manage. The speculative diagnosis was malnutrition and damaged lungs, possibly from floating gasoline or oil from nearby fishing boats. (Later findings confirmed avian tuberculosis; I was glad I'd been cautious about risking my indoor birds.) Vitamins and antibiotics were injected into a totally disinterested patient whose entire concentration was focused on just one more breath ... then another ... then one more....

As I drove slowly home, gently stroking his back, I felt sudden tremors shaking his body and, glancing down, I sensed a crisis. Pulling off the road, I stopped and gathered him into my arms, empathizing with his pain and longing to ease it. His head was down as he sucked in each breath with acute desperation, expelled it violently, and raspingly sucked in the next. Then, as though sensing the pain of my empathy, he turned his head on one side and his eye sought mine for a moment of deep, strangely evocative calm and understanding. It was a meeting of spirit with spirit, our outer forms with their disparate connotations falling away into their rightful irrelevance.

The expression froze: the depth in his eyes suddenly glazed to a shallow opacity as the dreadful suffering mercifully ceased.

With a swift, incredible illumination, I felt an enormous uprush emanating from the stilled feathers, rising and expanding in a glorious surge, swelling upwards and outwards beyond the trifling physical confines of a steel truck and filling the unbounded sky with imperishable, almost palpable vitality before disappearing.

Left behind was a human touched to the quick by the beauty and power of a released spirit returning to the light.

In the linoprint *Ascent,* the dying gull below, with his stilled eye fixed upon the viewer, is surmounted by rising interwoven energies as his spirit soars above.

In the painted version *The Supreme Liberation,* the invincible spirit we all share not only rises to the light in rhythms visually suggesting infinity but appears in flight as a tiny bird within the eye which is also an egg, symbolizing the potential of another beginning.

This intense experience continued to resurface in innumerable images of spiritual transcendence with varied bird forms rising out of metaphors of physical and psychological decay. A canvas entitled *The Crucible* is an example: deep in our watery depths, beginnings (expressed as 'alpha' fish) and endings (the Omega nebula) of *prima materia* pass through the fiery sacrifice of shedding the inessential (a process symbolized by the coral-coloured antler) to rise transfigured into a radiant unified bird/cross form on a higher spiritual plane.

In *The Dreamer,* our longing to transcend each particular level often seems fixed in immovable stone—here expressed by a supplicating Northwest Coast rock carving surmounted by expanding fiery growth and a soaring spiritbird.

Transcending bird forms eventually emerged poised over symbols of unacceptable attitudes that are spiritually, culturally and environmentally detrimental to all beings. In *Precarious Balance,* the rigid city skyline, so expressive of conformity, is causing its own disastrous upheaval. The promise of a new energy, a new consciousness, is shown in the glowing seed held in preservation in the bill of a spiritbird—a precarious balance between extremes.

CHAPTER TEN

From Ducks to Pigeons

OVER THE YEARS, ducks have always been favourites of mine but 'Rubble' was extra special. I grew closer to her than to any other duck, lovable as they all were, but our potential experience together hung by a thread—Rubble nearly wasn't born.

In twiggy seclusion one March near a small pond, a Rouen Duck patiently brooded her eggs week after week. When the pinnacle of her labours was reached and the nest overflowed with eleven downy babies, she led them down to the pond to safety.

For reasons known only to herself, she left one unhatched egg in the nest.

Nearby danger may have precipitated her departure. Perhaps she felt that eleven babies were enough for any mother at one time. Her owner found the cooled egg and quickly set it in an incubator where, undaunted by maternal rejection, Rubble soon emerged. Two days later when I was visiting, I was smitten by the beauty and charm of the tiny duckling with the obviously unquenchable personality. With very little persuasion, I took her home with me.

From the first time I'd heard the lilting architectural term 'wattle-and-daub,' I had envisioned the comical antics of bustling ducks rather than walls of woven sticks packed with clay. Consequently, I already had two adult ducks named 'Wattle' and 'Daub.' In searching for another architectural term for the new duckling, in order to keep a sense of 'family,' I finally settled on Rubble. It seemed more visually expressive of a duck's bill rubbling through leafy litter in search of bugs than a type of stone wall.

Rubble and I were together constantly. This was necessary in the beginning because she needed extra warmth continually with her higher body temperature and would stay snuggled inside my sweater. But we simply loved being together.

She slept on towels in a styrofoam box fitted with a heat lamp all set beside my bed. The first morning, I discovered that she'd soaked herself in her water dish and was chilled. Only ducklings living with their mothers are waterproof; the oil from the parents' glossy plumage is continually transmitted to the ducklings' down by contact. Also, their waterproofing is enhanced by static electricity developed by rubbing against the parents' feathers, while adults renew their electricity by frequent preening. Orphans like Rubble must not get wet until old enough to oil their own feathers. So I lifted her into bed with me and she cozied down on my chest under the covers till she was warm and dry.

When I worked my long weekend shifts at the university library, Rubbie went with me, spending most of the time peeking out of my sweater to the great amusement of the students. Ducks are very gregarious and ducklings, especially, need nurturing beyond food and water, so constant interaction was crucial to Rubble's well-being and development—I couldn't possibly have left her at home.

When I needed to coax her to sleep in the crook of my arm so that I could do the required paperwork, I would look down at her watching me and close my eyes drowsily for longer and longer intervals. Soon her playfulness would peter out and she'd be sound asleep by suggestion. Then I'd hurriedly scramble through my duties.

I often set her down into her box to eat or drink but if she suddenly lost sight of me, she'd spring out like a grasshopper. One of my most frequent duties was to fix the photocopier whenever it jammed and Rubbie quickly learned its whereabouts. Whenever I sneaked away to attend to it, she'd abandon her meal, leap out of the box and come thudding after me, squeaking with distress. The grins on hefty football students crowded around the malfunctioning copier still brighten my recollections, but their oft-repeated "What is it?" gave me serious doubts about higher education.

A previously-arranged commitment involving a day in Halifax now, of course, included Rubble. The night before the trip, I lay upstairs overtired from my two library shifts (one of fourteen hours duration, the other of ten), plus the non-stop care of Rubbie and found myself unable to sleep. Then I remembered how Wattle and Daub, when settling themselves to sleep, would slow their breathing to a long intake of air, a pause of two or three seconds, then an abruptly-released exhalation. I imitated the same breathing technique, found myself yawning within seconds, and blissfully fell asleep. Early the next morning, with Rubble tucked into my jacket and her foodbox on the seat beside me, I was off to Halifax.

Halfway there, I bought a coffee for myself and a muffin to share with Rubble. Passing eyebrows rose in disbelief as we munched it together in the parked truck. In a Halifax specialty store where I bought gourmet coffee for a friend, the saleslady was so entranced by her downy customer that she insisted on cuddling her and was loath to let her go. When I stopped in at the Art College Library, I set Rubble down on the floor for a little exercise, carefully fencing her into a short aisle of bookshelves while I made my selection. The space allotted her was too small for her high spirits and she persistently tried to dodge past me to the large, central sitting area where several students were reading and dozing. I foiled each attempt so adroitly that the little imp feigned indifference till I was stretching up for a book on the top shelf. In a flash she had zipped past and was out squeaking among the lethargic students with me in hot pursuit.

Fortunately, eccentricity is a carefully cultivated norm in art colleges, so hardly anyone dared to notice.

Later, I slipped into a small Mexican restaurant for a spicy, energizing meal before tackling the late afternoon traffic pouring out of the city. Luckily, I was the only customer. The waiter set a placemat before me with cutlery and a large glass of water. As he turned away, Rubble poked her head out of my jacket, spotted the water and strained forward eagerly, her outstretched bill nibbling in anticipation. I held the glass up to her and she instantly plunged her bill in excitedly, sucking water up noisily and squirting it out everywhere through her strainers. Then she submerged her whole head and blew loud gurgling bubbles ecstatically.

The waiter at the far counter was turned away from us but the gulping and sloshing easily reached his range of hearing. He grew rigid with disgust and closed his eyes but forebore to look at us. When he finally brought my meal from the kitchen, Rubble was again asleep inside my jacket and out of sight.

I faced him with what dignity I could muster over my sodden placemat and drenched clothes.

At the tollgate on the big suspension bridge spanning Halifax Harbour, I stopped long enough to fling my fare into the receptacle. The light switched to green but as I shifted gears, the transmission jammed. I tried repeatedly to dislodge it while the line of traffic behind me lengthened like an unwinding thread. Finally one of the attendants, a huge good-natured man, came over to check out the problem. I knew I could fix it by adjusting a lever inside the engine but the clutch had to be depressed at the same time. I explained the difficulty and he wedged himself in behind the wheel. Then I lifted a sleeping Rubble out of my jacket and handed her to him. His eyes widened.

"I need both hands," I said briefly, "hold her very carefully because she jumps."

Never will I forget those huge hands gently cradling one tiny duckling, the enormous grin linking the man's ears, the long line of traffic honking behind me, the emerging heads of drivers watching as I raised the hood and climbed up on the fender. Moments later we were speeding homeward triumphantly with the biggest grin I ever saw still following us like a beacon as the cars finally poured through the tollgate.

Halfway home, I stopped at a dairy bar for a revivifying ice cream cone while a squeaking Rubble, with her eager head peeking out of my jacket, enlivened the bored girls behind the counter. The final lap on a busy highway, defending my cone from a scrambling duckling determined to get her share, brought an exhausting day to a humorous close.

IN THE EVENINGS, I would stretch out on the couch with Rubble scampering up and down my front. One of her favourite games was to burrow under my sweater at the neck and push her way out through the sleeves—the final thrust at the wrists getting progressively more challenging as she grew bigger and bigger. When she was tired, she'd sprawl luxuriously on her tummy across my chest, her eyes happy but drowsy, her neck out in front and her legs straight out behind. I could rarely resist tickling her soft webs while she dozed contentedly.

As Rubble grew more mobile, she soon caught on to the advantages of being underfoot in the kitchen and was quick to grab any tidbits falling to the floor. Whenever she heard my voice at the back door as I returned from an outing, she'd run to meet me, squeaking her excitement. Soon her developing quack confirmed that she was a female; drakes have muted, mellow voices.

Rubble and I were inseparable outside and she'd pad patiently along behind me as I dug sods in the pasture and carried them up to the house to start a small lawn. Tirelessly she followed as I lugged armloads of weeds to the compost and cut a little path through the spruce trees to the meadow. I still call it 'Rubble's Path.'

Great was my consternation one day when I turned to see her nibbling wild mushrooms, but even holding her upside down failed to retrieve them. Fortunately, she took no harm. For a special treat, I'd carry her to a swampy dell in the woods which glowed with rich, mossy roots and overhanging greenery. Her unrestrained delight dabbling in the interlacing pools of water and churning up silt and bugs easily justified my chilled limbs as I sat nearby in the bitter spring breezes. Her thick down was impervious to discomfort.

She refused to let me out of her sight and one of my brightest images of her I caught by chance when I glanced down behind me late one afternoon. Rubble was following me on a sun-dappled path thickly carpeted with russet spruce needles and flanked with luminous greenery. Low shafts of rich sunlight touched her from behind, edging her downy innocence with golden glory as she peered up at me, an unforgettable radiant moment in the universal mosaic.

Rubble quickly developed a passion for garden bugs and loved foraging for them in the small flower beds surrounding the house. One day, while she was happily 'rubbling' and I was enjoying tea a few feet away in the porch, disaster nearly struck. She suddenly squawked with fright and I turned my head just as she dodged under the step. At that same instant, a Sharp-shinned Hawk crashed into the shrubbery beside us, tore himself loose and soared back up into the sky. It was a very close call.

When Rubble was nearly two months old, I decided that the time had come for her to sleep out in the pen with Wattle and Daub. All three were females and harmony prevailed whenever they were together. Rubble, not having been consulted, was appalled at this upheaval and scuttled back and forth in the pen quacking her protests. I watched from the house window in case of any conflicts but although Rubble continued to complain, the others settled down normally. In time, she adjusted to staying out and enjoyed accompanying Wattle and Daub on their daily forays, but most of each day we still spent together.

I was greatly amused at her efforts to imitate adult duck ways now that she had constant avian role models to follow. The ease with which Wattle and Daub stood, each on one leg and perfectly motionless, with their heads under their wings and their eyes shut, tantalized Rubble persistently. Over and over she tried to do the same but always her sagging adolescent crop would topple her forward.

Finally, she hit upon the perfect solution.

On a soft, drowsy afternoon, I was sitting out on the low deck at the back of the house enjoying my tea in company with the ducks and various wild birds. Wattle and Daub were nearby each standing on one leg asleep while Rubble strove, unsuccessfully as usual, to imitate their nonchalant pose. To my great mirth, she suddenly stalked over to the deck, propped her Mae West bosom up on the edge to steady herself, thrust one leg up under her feathers and triumphantly slipped her bill under her wing. Then she closed her eyes. The only element missing was the ease of long practice.

Wattle and Daub tolerated their younger companion in most ways but, being quiet ducks themselves, found her irrepressible chatter a bit much at times. Then, with consummate skill, they'd give her the slip. I'd hear Rubble's quacks of desertion ringing out as she circled the house calling for them while from the window I'd see the culprits padding silently down the road to the swamp without a backward glance.

She also had a genius for getting into dangerous difficulties. Each situation could have had serious consequences had I not been a chance witness. Once, in a fright, she leaped through a vinyl net fence that was supporting climbing plants. She shot through one of the squares but, unbelievably, entangled one leg in the taut vinyl and hung there, squeaking her distress. Later that summer, I paused by a window to watch her happily rummaging the debris of the vegetable garden, her low outstretched neck probing the tangled growth. Within moments, she had a tightening noose of bindweed around her neck and was struggling wildly to free herself.

Rubble's joyful celebrations at the nearby lake became a neighbourhood byword. A floating dock attached to the shore by a boardwalk was a popular bathing spot for local swimming enthusiasts—of which Rubble was one.

She'd begin at the shoreline with several long, satisfying drinks in order, as one admirer put it, to wet the inside first. Then she'd wade in, swimming alongside as I walked out on the boardwalk. Suddenly, ecstasy would ignite her and she'd beat her wings in a frenzy, churning the water, and roll into her famous somersaults, splashing glittering arcs in all directions. Meanwhile, I'd loll on the gently-heaving dock with my feet in the water enjoying her frenetic exuberance. After the somersaults, she'd literally speed around in wild circles on the dazzling surface, quacking hysterically and propelling herself with beating wings and feet. At last she'd settle down and bob placidly on the waves, oiling her feathers. Finally, she'd swim over to me and I would raise my legs so that my feet came up under her webs. Rubble, balancing carefully, would walk along my legs to my lap, drench me with a good shake and join me in a happy hug. Then she'd stand beside me on the wharf, preening in the summer sunshine while the waves lapped gently below. She was a favourite with everyone.

One autumn day, a friend and I, with Rubble in the middle, paddled out onto the lake in a canoe which had seen better days. I was in the rear, supposedly steering, but in reality lost in the beauty of the surrounding hills. I came to with a jolt:

"Rubbie's swimming!"

"So?" queried the other paddler, without turning her head.

"But I haven't put her into the lake yet!"

The head spun around with a cry of dismay. Through an unnoticed hole, water had been seeping steadily and a happy Rubble was now in her element.

We non-ducks barely made it back to shore.

Other days, Rubble and I would picnic together. I'd pack a delicious lunch, not forgetting a container of fresh water for Rubble, and drive to the ocean. She was too big by then to slip into my jacket but loved to stand on my lap or on the passenger seat of the truck quacking her observations. She found the vastness of the ocean a little unnerving but revelled in picnic tidbits washed down with lots of water. Luckily for her, she remained oblivious of the disbelieving stares of more orthodox families further down the shore.

Rubble's first experience of snow was a joy to behold. A light snowfall blanketed the ground one brisk morning when she emerged from the hay-lined hutch and she paused on the brink, eyeing the white stuff suspiciously. But soon the snow was crisscrossed with webbed prints and later, when large soft flakes began to drift slowly down, she stretched up on tiptoe, grabbing at them again and again, and positively chuckling.

However, bitterly cold mornings met with the decided

disapproval of all three ducks and they were quite reluctant to withdraw their feet from the protective warmth of their feathers. I'd scatter an armload of hay over the snow for them to walk upon and set out grain. Then I'd break the ice out of their dish, fill it with warm water and watch dry thirsty bills plunge in gratefully while the steam wreathed about their heads in the frosty air.

This was not enough for Rubble. As soon as she'd drunk her fill, she'd clamber into my lap, bitterly complaining, as I crouched beside the dish. Then she'd snuggle into my arms and thrust her cold wet bill straight down into the dry warmth of my bare neck.

Friendship can bear much.

On milder nights when soft snow fell gently and steadily, the ducks would often choose to sleep outside the hutch while the snow mounted higher and higher. In the morning when I'd call, three mounds of snow would shake loose and three questioning dark heads arise.

When the temperature plummeted to exceptionally cold readings, I would lead the ducks into the woodshed adjoining the house. There, a tiny door was built low into the house wall whereby I could fill the inside woodbox from the shed instead of carrying countless armloads around to the door. The ducks would scramble through the little doorway into the woodbox which had already been emptied and lined with hay. Then I'd fasten the insulated door behind them.

Indoors, I'd leave the woodbox lid propped up so we could enjoy one another's company. The temperature down inside the woodbox was cooler than the living room but much warmer than outside. Dishes of food and water were available and periodically I'd shower them with the plant mister to their great delight.

During Rubble's first winter, her egg cycles began and although she laid beautiful sea-green eggs regularly over the next year and a half, she never became in the least maternally inclined. Each day until her egg came to its readiness, she became somewhat fretful and irritable, but as soon as the laying was past, she'd brighten up again.

I would reflect with amusement that neither of us enjoyed our respective cycles. We were both definitely career birds.

I LOST RUBBLE to wild predators when she was barely two years of age. She was irreplaceable.

I tried eventually to express her within the universal scheme as the bringer of a special kind of freshness, as vital as the living water with which ducks are so associated.

In the linoprint *The Ambassador*, a leafy growth of vitality radiates from Rubble's frontal form while between the spreading rings of light encircling her, a single fallen leaf, like a piece of eggshell, floats before her in tribute. Within her eye, the eternal interaction of yin and yang form interwoven embryos of endless beginnings. The whole image is cut in what I call my 'seed cuts,' tiny spots of potential and light.

In the painting *Omphalos* (illustrated), leafy coloured auras emanate from Rubble as she floats on the invisible waters of life pervading the entire universe and pricked by pinpoints of stars— the glimpses of our inner illumination and understanding. Her reflection is a sun, light on another level. The egg-shaped canvas echoes the imperishable spirit crossing a new threshold.

In the canvas *Even Darkness Responds to the Light,* dark forces of destruction hold sway and the spiraling energy of creativity, symbolized by a shell, struggles in its net-like bonds. Swimming toward the inner light, Rubble leads the way, her wake of renewal opening in a wedge behind her like a cosmic mountain of freshness and growth. Above, the winged spirit flees, a precious glowing seed held carefully in its bill—the promise rescued.

ONE SUMMER, a tiny Parula Warbler was brought to me in an ingenious fashion. I arrived home late one night and high in the rafters of the porch roof, away from predators, was a cardboard box. Attached was a note: 'Please fix this bird.'

He had lost the use of his legs but his spirit shone and his wings were sound, so I held hopes for his recovery. From the beginning, he had no fear of me, ate well and showed no sign of pain. He was an exceptionally cheerful, endearing creature and I always felt we were working together in the effort to restore his legs.

Several times a day, I'd set him in my lap and manipulate the legs, but his toes never managed to grip. I'd also hold him upright, supporting him under his wings so he could exercise, and he'd beat them with wild enthusiasm, his eyes shining. For seven or eight days we persevered together without any improvement in his legs. His eagerness to regain mobility never flagged but I feared the legs were permanently paralyzed.

Then one morning there was a definite change that I can only describe as an acceptance on his part that the damage was irreversible. He abruptly stopped eating and lost all interest in exercises. His eyes changed from being bright and in touch to an inapproachable inner preoccupation. As clearly as if he had spoken, I knew that he had decided to let go. By the next day, he had passed on.

Birds have an amazing ability to let go of life—an ability that a human must respect and accept. This is not the same as being defeated by injuries so that the non-stop effort to live is without avail. On the contrary, it is a conscious decision to seek the release of death as part of the journey. I am awed whenever I encounter it.

On another occasion, when I was painting, a young grackle struck the window at high speed even though there were deterring hawk silhouettes painted on the glass. I immediately ran outside to where he was struggling on the ground, his wings flailing, and scooped him up. Birds that have struck windows I usually cradle in my hands, giving them darkness, a little warmth, and security from predators until they've fully recovered. But this one was obviously seriously injured.

I quickly set an empty aquarium indoors beside the window, lined it with a soft towel and laid him inside, flapping frantically. His head was twisted downwards and he was unable to raise it. As he propelled himself around the aquarium with his strong legs, trying desperately to balance with spread wings, his head would get wedged into corners between the glass and the towel. I had to rescue him many times to keep him from suffocating.

The situation looked grim.

I put in seeds, with small hope that he could eat, but to my surprise he eventually managed to do it. The seeds had to be a certain depth to allow his beak to push clumsily in and grab mouthfuls. I didn't dare leave a container of water with him for fear he'd drown. Every couple of hours I'd hold one near his head and gently push in his beak a few times. He always drank thirstily.

After a day, I thought I detected a faint improvement in the positioning of his head, and after two days I was certain. The third day, he held his head nearly normally, but couldn't stand or walk and his overall coordination was somewhat spastic. By this time, he was definitely minding the limitations of the aquarium, so I decided to shift him to the carving studio. A table, with containers of seeds and mealworms and a shallow water dish, was set beside the window so that he could be in touch with outside birds. I still bedded him with towels, since newspapers were too slippery for his propelling actions. I also edged the table with a high cardboard wall to prevent his falling off. But as he steadily improved, I was able to dispense with the wall and, after rearranging the room for his own safety, gave him the freedom of the whole carving studio.

About a month after the mishap, I felt I could let the grackle return to his natural life. He could walk and fly, although his coordination was still less than perfect, but his evident longing for freedom was too strong to be ignored.

For days I watched him closely at the feeders, noting that his flying muscles were redeveloping quickly. This was crucial since he was back in the world of predators. Then, eight days after his release, I saw him walking on the ground looking weak and shaky—a drastic change.

Had he struck another window? Or been bumped by a passing car?

Baby Juncos, orphans in need.

Tiny Tim (Timmy), the goose who couldn't walk (above).

Whoot the Saw-whet Owl (left and facing page).

Rubble inside my sweater at the university library (above).

Photo of Rubble as an adult, used for The Omphalos *(left). In this painting, leafy auras of colours emanate from Rubble as she floats on the invisible waters of life pervading the universe. The encircling rings are pricked pinpoints of stars, bright glimpses of our inner illumination and understanding. Her reflection is a sun (light on another level) and the egg-shaped canvas echoes the imperishable spirit crossing a new threshold.*

The Omphalos, *acrylic on canvas.*

The only time Molly accepted Desmond's overtures (above).

The Parula Warbler who finally 'let go' (facing page, top).

Desmond and Molly as babes, drying after a bath
(facing page, bottom).

The pigeons perching on skulls (above) inspired numerous artworks.

Centre Calm, *acrylic on canvas, (top), inspired by a flash vision while I was driving on a moonlit night.*

The arrival of baby Cliff Swallows (top and above left).

Here, the rusty rump which distinguishes Cliff Swallows is visible and also the new tail feathers 'leafing out' (above).

*Arrival of Chip the juvenile grackle—his eyes are calm by now
but the missing plumage is a reminder of his earlier trials.*

Chip outside during the first attempt at release (above).

Chip 'anting' at high speed with onions (right).

Chip 'helping' with the firewood (left).

The aerodynamic grace and tiny feet of Flit, the Cliff Swallow (below).

After a scramble through the bushes, I caught him and rein-stated him in the carving studio. His coordination was again very poor and simply failed to improve. He was eventually reduced once more to pushing himself across towels rather than walking. He ate everything with enthusiasm but I began to realize that he could never be released again.

It was an even greater pity since he was only a juvenile bird experiencing his first summer season.

After a few weeks, he abruptly stopped eating and lay quietly by the hour gazing out of the window, his thoughts evidently elsewhere. I felt certain that he'd decided to let go and I couldn't help but agree with him, sad though it all was.

Two days later, he was lying on his front turned away from me. I glanced in at him and he turned his head toward me slightly, gently lifting one wing. Then he turned away and a few minutes later I heard a faint scuffling sound. When I looked again, he was lying on his back dead, as though the spirit in leaving had moved him in the same great upheaval as when he had broken out of his egg in the spring.

Each birth had been equally tremendous.

In the painting *The Song of the Spirit*, I have laid him within the primordial ocean above a hatching universe of spring foliage. The energies rise from his stilled form like sap to form the ubiquitous tree of life and death whose branches cascade in living waves of beginnings and endings. Within the trunk, a chrysalis of light releasing the spirit above is superimposed over the star-bright centre of wholeness with its transparent moth wings of waning and waxing cycles.

By juxtaposing these symbols of transcendence, I tried to express that letting go is not so much a striving for the next threshold as a letting go of this one, a necessary paring away for fulfilment—an acceptance of change.

Not all birds with permanent physical handicaps decide to let go. I once had a Bohemian Waxwing who'd lost half a wing to entertain an 'enlightened' boy with a BB gun. 'Icarus' lived with me for over a year in a small tree set up in my bedroom. Attached to the branches were halved oranges and cups of blueberries, cranberries and whatever other fruit was in season. The soft, high notes of his singing were intensely beautiful and gentle, and I marvelled at the magnificent adjustment he'd made to such a different lifestyle. Even more marvellous, at the opposite end of the same room, lived an adult crow moving freely between two freestanding perches, a table and some shelves. Not once did he ever interfere with the disabled waxwing but shared their altered lifestyles in complete harmony.

"WOULD YOU TAKE CARE of two baby pigeons till my husband gets back? They seem to be sick."

They were certainly in poor shape. Only ten days old, yet one had been battered and defeathered by the adult flock of Lahore Fancy Pigeons till his skin was bare with bloody patches. His eyes, though, looked bright and strong. The other sat listlessly hunched over with unhappy eyes and a hard, impacted crop. An antiseptic wash for the first and a dose of mineral oil followed by a crop massage for the other set the two of them back on their feet again. 'Desmond' and 'Molly' were on their way.

For feeding, I softened pigeon grain pellets and powdered vitamins with raw egg and warm water. Then I cupped my hand over the dish and gently pushed their heads into the narrow opening within my curved fingers. Baby pigeons don't gape for food like songbird nestlings but thrust their beaks into their parents' throats and are fed 'pigeon milk,' a curd-like secretion formed in the parents' crops. With my hands cupped around their beaks as they sought for food, I hoped to simulate a parental pigeon crop—an unusual personal aspiration.

The ruse worked.

Gradually, I found that I had only to cup my fingers over the dish to start them eating and that when I withdrew, they'd continue without me. Eventually, they tucked in as soon as they saw the food and, in time, were able to switch to dry pellets, mixed seeds, grit and water on their own. As they grew in health and confidence, I put up shelves for them on which they slept like city pigeons on downtown ledges; these gave them a secure home base from which they began to explore their surroundings.

The freedom of the house was theirs, and the warm sunlight gliding slowly across the floors proved irresistible. Side by side, they'd snuggle down contentedly in the brightness till the shadow crept over them. Then they'd rise, patter over to the light and nestle back down till the shadow caught up again.

Watching them basking and preening in a small glow of light surrounded by dusky forms planted visual seeds in the back of my mind that blossomed for years to come. Desmond emerged in the linoprint *The Shadow* cleaning his tailfeathers, oblivious of the threatening background, an image suggesting the urgency of maintaining one's purity of purpose in spite of the menace of approaching shadows and thereby effecting positive changes—as the dominant egg form suggests. In *Seeker of the Sun,* another linoprint, he symbolized the spirit that ever seeks the light in spite of the power of darkness to overwhelm.

Molly, dozing contentedly on one of my recumbent cow skulls, presented a provocative contrast between the spiritual and the physical which crystallized in an unexpected vision as I was driving to town one night. A low gibbous moon hovered ahead of me as I swung onto the highway. Suddenly, though my thoughts were entirely elsewhere, I saw overlaid against the dark sky a huge image of Molly lying on the cowskull, the actual moon eloquent above her.

I rendered her amid the unsettling atmosphere of an ambiguous, amoebe-like mackerel sky with a waning moon, a picture in which she evokes the security of the centre, that inner light among the shadows, that still point within the ever-increasing whirl. Molly's closed eyes emphasize the inner stillness opposing the outer activity and I entitled the canvas *Centre Calm* (illustrated).

As the pigeons matured into adults, Desmond began courting Molly. In the beginning she reciprocated his interest and the two displayed charming rituals of 'billing and cooing' and side-by-side strutting. Then suddenly, for reasons undecipherable to me, Molly abruptly squashed Desmond's advances and although Desmond persisted for years with his amorous aspirations, Molly never again welcomed them. Their lifelong domestic squabbles ever shone as a humorous refuting of the accepted lascivious reputation of pigeons.

Nevertheless, their daily lifestyle was so much calmer and freer of mischief than that of the various songbirds, ducks and roosters who have shared my life, that I was led to ruminations on their traditional association with peace in a world which seems never to have known it.

Crisis, *linoprint.*

They began to symbolize for me the spirit and its journey to fulfilment, the growth of inner strength through gentle interaction with the natural challenges of existence. In *Crisis* (illustrated), the driving spirit (personified by Molly) is forever engaged in seeking balance between the interacting opposites whose force in this piece is visualized by the traditional strength of the dragon. The polarity of waning and waxing crescent moons stress this duality but the light radiates from Molly's eye, the power of the centre. Perhaps Molly's unswervable resistance to Desmond's overtures suggested my placing her in the centre—the still point, the immovable.

On one occasion, Molly contributed a direct response to my meditations on natural rather than traditional images that could become metaphors for soulboats, those spiritual vessels that carry our life essence safely over the next threshold after death. I had decided that a curved, fallen leaf, associated with the transition of the seasons, would be an exciting possibility with a cargo of souls or embryos. As I sat pondering what else would be suitable, Molly, busily preening above me on her shelf, discarded a white curved feather which drifted gently down and landed in a gracefully-poised arch on the floor.

What better symbol of decay and renewal? Within days I had used the feather soulboat in a print and a painting.

Desmond came into his own when I was commissioned by the priest of Glendale, Cape Breton, to do a painting for the alter wall of his church. Father MacLeod desired a symbolic rendering of the Holy Spirit using a dove—truly a gift amongst commissions.

In an eight-foot circle of wholeness and eternity, *The Power and The Glory* (illustrated), Desmond rises forever resplendent in radiant wing and tail feathers, the sacred fish with star eyes of illumination flowing out to replenish our hearts, and soul stars glowing above. The interaction of opposites—the celestial with the terrestrial, the sacred with the profane, merge to form a vital cross radiating from the centre.

The baby pigeons who came 'temporarily' and remained a permanent part of my life enriched it beyond measure.

As I SAT PONDERING the succession of birds that I had tried to help over the years, I reflected yet again how deeply each encounter had enriched my life and art, and how I had always been blessed with a plethora of images through which to convey their teachings. Then my thoughts hovered around Puck and her sudden departure, and I wondered what further avian adventures awaited me.

The very next morning I heard about 'Chip.'

CHAPTER ELEVEN

An Irrepressible Grackle

WORD HAD COME TO ME about a baby starling taken in by well-intentioned people. Both adults in the family were at work all day, the bird was confined to a small cage in a closed room because of five prowling housecats, and was being fed primarily dog food and worms by the children—when they remembered. Puck hadn't been gone long so I was especially sensitive to any situation concerning starlings and I worried about this one. Finally, I paid a visit with an offering of mealworms (and five cat collars with attached mini-cowbells) only to discover, not a starling in the cage, but a two-week old grackle.

The parents were busy, friendly folk who had a real concern for the welfare of the bird. They also understood the necessity of 'belling' their cats and graciously accepted the collars. Upon learning that the youngster would require a lengthy initiation into the elements of survival, they were relieved to pass him over to me. And, as usual, I was delighted to take him on. I tucked him into my shirt, climbed into the van amidst waving goodbyes and drove home.

Chip's confinement and his irregular feeding schedule (he hadn't been fed for over two hours when I first saw him) had stressed him so acutely that he'd cry loudly at each word I spoke, having associated the human voice with food. Although he began tentatively feeding himself mealworms the first day, I still handfed him worms and mixed bugs when he gaped. However, I was unable to leave a large quantity of mealworms available for him since he would gobble them all at once. His irregular feedings had induced extreme anxiety and he was unable to leave any food uneaten. He was the only bird I've ever known who was in danger of overfeeding himself. From the first, I regulated his meals with great precision in order to help stabilize him. His eyes were full of apprehension and his appetite absolutely enormous but as he responded to constant affection, attention and predictable feedings, his confidence grew, his eyes became calmer and the danger of overeating ceased.

Chip's coordination, too, was behind his age but with the freedom of the house I felt that this problem would quickly disappear. His tail feathers had been badly splayed from the cage bars and he was terribly smelly but he learned to bathe by his second day. Almost immediately, his feathers became sleek and he smelled as fresh and sweet as a normal bird.

Bubble and Squeak, as I expected, were gentle with the little stranger, allowing him to land on their backs, and Bubble even carefully removed a fleck of food from Chip's beak. All four of us would sit together in an armchair in the screened porch, enjoying the sweet-scented early summer evenings. Once Squeak, out of curiosity perhaps, peered down closely into Chip's face only to have Chip suddenly gape up at him hopefully—an engaging image. When the roosters stood up at intervals to shake and preen, Chip would investigate their feet, perching on their large toes or pecking curiously and innocently at their long, threatening spurs.

Chip was soon in charge of his own feedings and eventually began to reject earthworms—an ultimatum I get sooner or later from every fledgling. However, a dish of mealworms and another of mixed bugs were acceptable. He was greatly intrigued by my own meals, sampling everything off my tongue and rejecting very little—unlike fastidious Puck. Friends arriving for breakfast one morning had little choice about sharing their pancakes with Chip and he topped off a satisfying repast by a lengthy sunbath on one visitor's shoulder.

Chip also had a curious habit of accepting a series of tidbits from my tongue until he could eat no more. The he'd take a final piece, decide he simply couldn't manage it, and fly off and leave it somewhere—often dropping it behind the couch. This was probably residual behaviour from his earlier caged days. In time, I began to discover strange, wizened, sometimes mouldy objects that were wholly unidentifiable flourishing in peculiar places.

Chip loved to be with me, no matter what I was doing, and would even nestle down in a warm heap against my neck and doze despite the hideous roar of the vacuum cleaner I was wielding. He never showed the least inclination to snuggle inside my shirt as Puck had done, but then grackles are raised in open nests, not treeholes. When I decided to re-paint the studio for the first time since I'd built it, Chip slept cozily on my shoulder while I eased myself down, painfully erect, to dip the brush, rose again slowly and then painted carefully so as not to disturb him. Half an hour of such slow, steady, deep knee bends would surely be beneficial to my physical well-being, I moaned inwardly.

Chip's playfulness, however, really set him apart. Seen through his eyes, toys came in a multitude of shapes and sizes, and he carried the most surprising array of objects all over the house. A measuring tablespoon without a handle, jar lids, a plastic electric plug insert, a beer cap, pencils (especially fun to grab by the eraser end), a tiny spoon used to measure the pigeons' vitamin powder (and which I never did recover), plastic clothes pegs, a foam and metal finger splint, a piece of lightweight chain, sea shells, and dried Chinese lanterns. Bells were a special delight and he'd pick them up and ring them vigorously. Openwork cat toys with bells inside were so entertaining for him that I suspended a couple by strings and he rang them constantly trying to detach them. One day the lens cap from my camera flew past my face— with Chip excitedly propelling it from the rear.

In time, I set aside a charming clay animal planter, filled (and continually refilled) it with his motley collection of toys and considered it Chip's toy box—the only grackle of my acquaintance to have one. Only to select friends did I admit to emerging from a toystore having paid hard-earned money for a livid green rubber tarantula with hairy legs that squealed hideously when pinched. Chip loved it.

AT THIS TIME, my reclusive habits were due for a major upheaval. A CBC film crew was scheduled to shoot a day's footage at my house in order to produce a short documentary on my artwork. I had done my best to attain an acceptable standard of orderliness and cleanliness, consoling myself the while with timely reminders that the format desired was the artist 'in situ.'

The dreaded day arrived and with it a pair of stalwart friends for moral support; a camera man and a sound man, both loaded with intimidating equipment; and a producer who was allergic to feathers.

However draining I may have found the experience, to the birds it was exhilarating. Desmond and Molly, stimulated by the confusion of people and equipment in a normally quiet studio, flew time and again in front of the camera and cooed almost continuously over the sound track, necessitating innumerable retakes. Desmond, in particular, became so insistent on monopolizing centre stage that he had to be banished eventually to the carving studio at the far end of the house. Birds landed over and over on the various heads milling below them and during one take, the allergic producer sat with streaming eyes, valiantly suppressing chokes just off camera, while Molly perched on her head and Chip played in her lap.

Chip also busied himself tugging wires and plugs from the audio equipment and arousing justifiable wrath in the sound man who kept picking up discordant interference through his earphones. As well, Chip terrified us all, whenever we were in danger of making progress, by trying to land on the various searing-hot lights and reflectors that were capable of sizzling his toes to a crisp. Fortunately for what was left of everyone's peace of mind, he finally chose to help out in the kitchen making sandwiches and sampling tantalizing treats of avocado and cheese.

During lunch break the camera man, perhaps to escape the turmoil inside, took a quiet stroll outside under the trees only to get attacked from the rear by an indignant Squeak defending his territory. Indeed, I wondered if the camera would accrue more entertaining footage if, instead of pointing so persistently and belligerently at me, it peered out from behind me at everyone else.

In the end, all the birds were included in the show, perhaps because they were unavoidable, and Chip, in a charming sequence destined to nauseate the more fastidious viewers, was filmed eating bits of sodden cracker off the tip of my trembling tongue.

The day following the film shoot, I decided to try launching Chip into the outdoor world. Accordingly, at seven a.m., I sat on the back deck consoling myself by hugging the roosters and watching Chip up in the trees. He was now about five weeks of age and beginning to moult his juvenile plumage but I still hadn't convinced him to eat wild birdseed. I was concerned, too, about his trusting attitude towards humans and wondered if he'd imprinted on his previous foster parents. My experience with various songbirds through the years has seen their trust with other humans gradually diminish, their trust in me being the last to go. Our house, in its woodland setting, was surrounded daily at that time by a host of adult and juvenile grackles as well as other wild birds. I hoped that Chip would learn their ways and their unequivocal distrust by imitation and association. I went back inside so that the waiting throng, chucking warnings up in the trees, could fly down and resume feeding.

Several hours later, I emerged only to have Chip fly instantly to my shoulder crying urgently for food. I fed him mealworms and then watched in amusement as he saucily chased a chipmunk under the deck until the chipmunk remembered his dignity and chased him back. At suppertime, I brought Chip back inside where he again wolfed down several mealworms and retired immediately to a corner of the carving studio for a sound sleep of an hour and a half's duration. Outdoor life was evidently exhausting.

The next day followed much the same procedure but Chip was too trusting and unaware outside, as though danger from hawks was non-existent. He showed no interest in other grackles or in eating grain and he preferred to play instead of hunt for food. At one point, when I was napping upstairs, wearied from watching him and worrying, he roused me by tapping on the window, so I brought him back inside.

He simply wasn't ready to be on his own.

Indoor life definitely encouraged Chip's ingenious playfulness. He added a dish of cello-wrapped candies to his toy list, tossing them into the air to roll down his back and carrying them all over the house. He rolled them repeatedly down cushions as well, chasing them and carrying them back to the top to start again. The perforated metal trap normally lodged in the drain of the kitchen sink was another lodestone that reappeared from one end of the house to the other. Often, when he was thirsty, he'd tweak up the spout cover of the electric kettle and poke his head in for a drink. This feat presented such nightmarish images in my mind as burned tongues and melted beaks that whenever I boiled water, standing guard the while, I immediately cooled the unused hot water with cold.

Reasonably hot water flowing from the tap intrigued Chip and he'd grab mouthfuls of it and thrust it among his feathers as though 'anting'—that mysterious ritual whereby birds push ants in under their plumage, possibly because the acid secreted by the ants deters parasites.

Once when I was peeling a bowlful of tiny Egyptian onions, halving only the largest, Chip persisted in standing up to his belly in them, rubbing himself with peeled onions and thrusting them in among his feathers. Onions stuck out of his plumage everywhere, shot out when he shook himself, or fell to the floor when he flew. He was so excited as he grabbed and thrust the slippery little things that they'd hurtle out of his beak and roll crazily in all directions over the counter like a frenzied game of billiards.

Chip's devilish nature rapidly developed as well. He quickly learned to ensure my undivided attention by suddenly pinching one of the freckles on my neck with excruciating accuracy. Usually I was eating at the time and when I'd whip my head around and glare ferociously at him on my shoulder, he'd gape innocently for food. In time, I began to keep a package of his favourite crackers by my chair so that when he pinched a freckle for food (inducing me to feel like a vending machine) and I was buried under sleeping chickens or engrossed in a book, I could simply reach for a cracker, soften it in my mouth and offer bits on my tongue. If occasionally I didn't respond, he'd keep tweaking freckles as though trying for the 'right' one. I began to wonder if I might develop flashing lights and 'empty' signs.

Another frustrating aspect of Chip's personality was his manic drive to shred every cherished houseplant I owned. I covered the most frequently-abused smaller ones with window screening but the larger ones were at his mercy. He knew perfectly well that I objected so he diabolically chose to shred them when, again, the chickens were slumbering peacefully in my lap and I was loath to disturb them. I'd start my protests by hurling threats, which he refused even to acknowledge. Then I'd proceed to a series of denunciations on a rising scale of exasperation, and finally sling crackers to distract him. Once, in sheer frustration, I threw the entire box of crackers—and broke a plant. Usually, I'd end up distracting the roosters instead, who'd climb down to investigate the crackers. When I'd finally get to my feet, Chip would invariably land on my shoulder and in response to my bared teeth and glittering eye, gape winningly for crackers.

I eventually resorted to grinding black peppercorns over the leaves and a truce was established in time for some of the more promising remnants to recover.

Chip's love of crackers suggested an easy way to treat him with tetracycline. He'd been bothered with a lingering sneezy cough and I hoped finally to rout it. However, he quickly realized which cracker tidbits were medicinal and he'd drop them behind the couch before asking for more. Often, when I was away from home, I'd return to find the package of crackers hammered into holes with pieces and crumbs scattered everywhere. Indeed, our lifestyle could be said to be 'crackers.'

Chip's mischievous curiosity occasionally extended to other unfortunates besides myself. Three women, two of them strangers, arranged to visit me one day and were duly greeted outside by the roosters—who were always tolerant of new 'hens.' Next, they were introduced to Molly on top of the bathroom door and Desmond in the studio. Then I called Chip in from the living room. He landed on my hand with a visible start as he spotted the three strangers and I was surprised to finally note this more guarded attitude towards humans.

His way of sizing them up was fascinating. After eyeing them carefully for a moment, he flew onto the head of the first and paused motionlessly for a long moment. Then he flew onto the head of the second, paused once more, and flew on to the third. It was impossible not to infer that he was 'reading' and assessing them, perhaps by the transmission of their energies.

Once they'd met with his approval, he relaxed and began tugging their earrings, pulling eyeglasses, pinching toes in openwork sandals, poking into their ears and eyes, prying under watches, rooting brazenly through their hair and indiscriminately dispensing droppings.

I informed my bewildered guests that they should feel honoured by Chip's unqualified acceptance.

As the first of August drew near, I decided with amusement to have a birthday party for Bubble and Squeak—mainly, I admit, because I had a new cake recipe that promised to be mouthwatering and calorie-friendly. I invited a couple of friends, no crazier than I, who threw themselves wholeheartedly into the humour of the situation.

One of them found herself pondering the selection of birthday cards available in a local drugstore, trying to find one suitable to give to roosters. While there, she encountered a garrulous acquaintance who naturally enquired about the recipient of the card. The embarrassed friend was slippery enough to make her escape without giving a direct answer.

Both guests eventually arrived on party day bearing gifts of raisins and shredded coconut for Bubble and Squeak. Meanwhile, I had baked the boys a quickbread loaded with raisins and white millet and topped with two candles. I'd also baked a more human-oriented concoction liberally iced on top which was enjoyed by all.

Two years previously on that day Squeak had hatched in the dining room while twelve-hour-old Bubble and I had cheered him on.

A fortnight later, another acquaintance arrived on the doorstep with two tiny nestlings huddled together in a contrived nest of soft dried grass.

CHAPTER TWELVE

Windrider

THE NEW ARRIVALS were exceptionally tiny but although their beaks, as usual, were disproportionately wide at the base, they were oddly minute from base to tip. The plumage was dark on their heads and backs, and muted white edged with grayish-brown on their breasts. Their throats were spotted dark and white, but their beautiful fawn rumps held the key to their elusive identity at last—I had never before seen baby Cliff Swallows.

They had been gallantly rescued from a young boy fully determined to keep them as pets. With whimsical tufts of down still adhering to their juvenile plumage and inch-long emerging tail feathers still partially sheathed, I tentatively estimated their age at ten days to two weeks.

Immediately upon their arrival I was plunged once more into weeks of hunting for bugs to feed them, severely hampered by their adamant rejection of earthworms. Normally, of course, baby swallows would be fed only flying insects caught by their soaring parents and although my spirit was willing, my flesh was flightless. These babies had to content themselves with my standard nestling fare of sowbugs, centipedes, spiders, mealworms and, when available, cabbage worms. When unavoidable bits of dirt or bark encrusted their food, I couldn't dismiss the humorous notion that they wanted me to know this wasn't the way mother had always presented supper.

With the hot August weather rapidly drying the land, I was forced several times to transport my charges to other buggier locales in hopes of satisfying them. As I'd crouch by the hour turning over rocks and chunks of wood, I developed, in desperation, such a spontaneous snatch at anything that moved that, one morning, I hurled a small, unsuspecting salamander straight into the bucket before I fully realized what it was.

Another time, after I'd turned over a short log and cornered the inhabitants, I scrambled hopefully through a clump of leafy litter. To my great consternation, out tumbled several blind velvety baby shrews. Fortunately, the mother was away and I carefully replaced her family and covered them once again.

Yet another day, I returned home from foraging to find that some kind soul had left a bag hanging on the doorknob with three containers inside. My hopes soared that they contained bugs for the babes but my disappointment was tempered by the delight of finding them full instead of succulent wild blueberries for me.

The swallows were the easiest nestlings to keep clean because they never fouled their 'nest.' I took a small mixing bowl, half-filled it with a folded towel and on this placed a shallow basket which overlapped the rim of the bowl. In the basket, I laid a large, thick woolly sock, on which the babies lay, and arched another protectively over the top of them, holding it in place with curved pipecleaners. This gave them a warm, covered nest with enough room to manoeuver their tails over the edge to defecate while clinging to the basket. As their surprisingly noxious droppings were expelled with considerable force, a newspaper in front of the bowl accommodated their 'firing range.'

Chip's initial reaction was jealousy and he snapped at the babes several times so I plied him with extra attention and special tidbits which reassured him. Thereafter, I could trust him alone with them when I was out hunting bugs. Occasionally, he'd land on top of their nest, mischievously pressing the roof down on their heads, but this device was more to provoke me than to threaten the babes. His primary focus was to infiltrate their bug supply and he was quick to discover the bucket hidden in the darkened bathtub behind the shower curtain. If he was successful in snitching a bug, he'd dance about just out of my reach, clutching it and daring me to chase him. His greatest delight seemed to be in getting away with something.

This was his latest development and often I'd chase him, mimicking dire threats, while he dodged around eluding my 'grabs.' If I truly wanted him out of the way momentarily, I had only to drop some enticing object near him and casually reach for it. Chip, with devilish glee radiating from every feather, would snatch it up first, gloating, and I'd 'chase' him out of the room. Then I'd quickly complete whatever task was only possible without his harrowing energies—like pouring bubbly, hot jam into clean bottles.

The new babies were very difficult to feed for the first couple of days until they began to associate me with food and volunteered to gape. Until then, I'd hold each tiny head steady, slip my fingernail gently between their minute mandibles, pry them apart and, theoretically at least, push in the bug. More often the bug by that point had slithered out of my grasp, or would re-emerge from their mouths stuck to my finger, or would be snatched away at the eleventh hour by Chip—who grabbed faster than one could believe possible. One feeding session could last fifteen minutes.

When the babes finally began to gape, conveniently chirping their hunger every thirty minutes, I sent up a fervent prayer of gratitude to every known deity.

Bubble and Squeak showed no jealousy whatsoever; Squeak especially seemed almost paternally gentle. The first time I fed the babies with the roosters reposing in my lap, Bubble, who as usual was furthest away, merely stood up in order to see better while Squeak simply turned his head to watch and remained lying quietly.

Desmond and Molly were unimpressed. In their eight and a half years, they'd seen it all.

From the beginning, one of the swallows had a very slight sniffly cough which didn't concern me unduly as he was always bright-eyed and hungry. So many nestlings I've known, including Puck, have developed a similar sound which eventually disappeared. However, after a week, he suddenly began to breathe solely through his mouth and his back appeared to be slightly humped. I immediately began treating him by dipping either the tip of my finger or a mealworm into a tetracycline-based antibiotic before placing it in his mouth—cursing myself meanwhile for not having begun sooner. Soon I had to devise other ways of sneaking the medicine down his throat since, as soon as he suspected its presence, he'd refuse to open his mouth. I stubbornly persisted but he showed no improvement. In fact, his humped look seemed more pronounced.

Two days later in the evening, when he turned his head, I noticed with horror a large transparent swelling on his back above his left wing and behind his neck. Veterinarians evaporate after office hours so after a hurried consultation by telephone with a more scientifically-minded friend, I fitted a scalpel with a new blade, immersed it in fast-boiling water and slashed the swelling. I had expected blood, pus or perhaps a parasitic larva—but not air.

The swelling instantly deflated. The little babe, in contrast to my rattled state of mind, seemed positively rejuvenated by his harrowing experience and immediately began preening. His appetite, which had been poor for a few hours, also picked up.

Further consultations with my friend, as well as with a vet the following morning, led us to the conclusion that one of the air sacs had been damaged by rough handling—probably by the original boy. The skin would seal very quickly but should another swelling arise, the damage would be considered irreversible. I continued with the tetracycline.

Sadly, two-and-a-half days later, the little one refused his morning feedings and very shortly died. I believe that he was granted a gentle passing because he still lay normally in the nest with his head drooping down over the edge. Examination of his plumage revealed another smaller swelling of air hidden in the feathers.

The second of the cliff swallows had also endured emergency treatment earlier on the same day that I had 'operated' on the first. I had left the two babes in the care of the same friend at the university, where she is the Animal Care Technician, while I combed her home yard for bugs. During the first feeding, she noticed the smaller nestling experiencing difficulty in swallowing and, as he gaped, she could just detect something black on the tongue. She pried open the tiny beak with one set of tweezers and with another removed in pieces a large, dead carpenter ant. Centipedes, carpenter ants and other stinging food sources have to be killed just prior to being pushed into nestlings' throats. Apparently, this one hadn't been quite dead when I'd fed the babe earlier and had bitten into the back of the tongue and died there. Fortunately, my friend is cool-headed and skilful in such situations. I would have needed extra time just to descend from the ceiling.

Each moment consists of dying and renewal. The morning the first little cliff swallow passed on, exactly two weeks after their arrival, saw the second glorying in the exhilaration of flying. I was amazed at how easily 'Flit' flew—with none of the blundering and crash landings I've usually experienced with fledglings. He flitted through the rooms with the soft flutter of a bat. Had there been wind indoors, his flight would have been soundless. By this point, his wings in repose reached the tip of his tail, his whole body was incredibly streamlined and his dark plumage had a low lustre. In essence, his entire body was a wing. When he first land-ed on me, I was amazed at the unbelievably soft touch of his arrival—most unlike Chip's ebullient thump and vigorous grip. When I considered Flit's minute size (much smaller than a budgie) and his seeming fragility, I marvelled that he was perfect-ly capable of migrating further than Brazil and back again— although it seemed as if a hearty sneeze could get him as far as Mexico.

With Flit daily becoming more mobile, I decided to supply flying insects for him so he could learn to become a 'real' swallow. He was still being handfed, although if I were patient, I could coax him to pick up a bug from my hand rather than having to push it into his throat. However, it was always up to me to initi-ate the feedings.

Accordingly, I drove one day to a riding stable where a friend boarded her horse and we quickly developed an efficient system of catching barn flies. She'd back each horse out of its stall, cross-tie it in the corridor and stride around the stall maniacally flailing a small nylon net in figure eights. Suddenly, she'd stop and choke the net with her free hand, I'd lift the lid off a large jar, she'd press in the writhing mass of flies and I'd instantly recap the bottle. Our captured flies steadily increased from stall to stall but our bizarre activities also pushed a wave of anxiety before us. Horses, whose turns were upcoming, began nervously jerking their heads and rolling their eyes over the partitions while each cross-tied beast suspiciously eyed the whirling, whistling net with alert ears and uneasy fascination.

Not one of the puzzled humans who witnessed our intensive fly frenzy dared to question us.

Climbing into the van, I gloated over the two big jars of milling, buzzing flies but as I lifted the greenish antique one looking for my keys, the thin glass suddenly snapped apart and a black whirlwind of flies stormed out before I could clamp it together again. Masking tape was hastily applied but days passed before I could drive without dozens of the denizens zooming distractingly around my head.

Flit seemed quite unimpressed by my hardwon booty, some of which I released within the screened porch for his delectation. The rest I stored in the fridge to hibernate until they were needed. He mustered only a tepid interest in watching them, so I tried to stimulate his hunting instincts—if only to rest my own. I fed him sparingly so he'd be hungry and locked Chip, who revelled in snapping at flies, out with him as a role model.

Periodically, I killed flies for Flit, holding each squashed cadaver before his beady eyes so he'd connect the plethora of live flies, crawling revoltingly all over my bare arms, with food. He'd eat the carcasses with evident enjoyment but then his interest would abruptly cease. He simply wasn't ready for that next step. Perhaps, as well, the small porch was too confining for the natural soaring and hunting so associated with eating within his ancestral memory.

Chip's jealousy, meanwhile, was still lurking below the surface and when I set Flit upon the branches out in the screened porch, Chip's annoyed swoopings made me suddenly realize that I was violating a territory he considered his own. This necessitated nailing up branches for Flit elsewhere. Chip also resented Flit landing on me and often flew just behind Flit, 'stalking' him through the air. Careful diplomacy was needed to smooth out all grievances.

Flit, so new to the idea of landing on anything, would try to land cliffwise on my face, scrambling for a hold with his tiny sharp claws. Eventually, he learned that my shoulder or the top of my head still qualified as being me though hitherto his associations had been with my face and hands. In a short time, he'd 'trained' me to hold up my finger as he swung in for a landing. If I failed to be ready, he'd chirp sharply and pick up speed, circling and banking for another attempt like a little monoplane on a gusty day. In my more hysterical moments, I began mentally to design wind socks for the living room.

Flit's smug retort to Chip's aerial harassment was to hook cliffwise high onto the burlap-covered end wall of the cathedral living room. Chip was unable either to land on the wall himself or to intimidate Flit into letting go. Gripping tightly to my shoulder was very difficult, however, for Flit and he'd often tumble off and become airborne no matter how carefully I moved. His preference was to perch on my finger by the hour.

Flit also experimented with landing on Bubble's back and attempting to burrow into his feathers, when he wasn't landing on Bubble's enormous comb. The patience and gentleness of Bubble was an unending source of amazement to me.

Flit insisted on being with me at all times and I grew accustomed to managing nearly all my activities with one hand. He accompanied me upstairs to bed each night, refusing even to be parted long enough for me to undress. As I lay reading, he dozed on my head or on the book, until I was too tired to read any longer. Then I tried to peel him off and set him in the little tree over my bed. Even at that point, I had to be quick to switch off the light or he'd be back on my head in a flash.

In the glow of the nightlight (a device I find necessary with birds who so easily initiate emergencies in utter darkness) I could just discern Flit's roosting posture—his thick flank plumage projecting from each side like a portable nest and cradling his long slender wings, his tiny head tucked deeply into his feathers.

CHIP'S PLAYFULNESS continued to be as entertaining as ever and one hot afternoon saw him roguishly grabbing ice cubes out of my iced tea and flying off with them—obviously in the hopes that I'd want them back and would chase him. An arrangement of dried Chinese lanterns he picked apart to expose the seeds—then promptly devoured them.

Chip also had a distinctive touch with apples: shredding one all over a newly-primed canvas and leaving the bits to darken and stick to the surface was the work of a moment for him. One evening found him up on the woodbox with half an apple brazenly stolen from the chickens. There he proceeded systematically to break off chunks and toss them down to the roosters circling below, who devoured each piece as it fell at their feet. Another day, when I was cutting up apples to make applesauce, he delighted in snatching at the knife as it sliced and in one horrible instance, which is permanently seared on my memory, caught his lower mandible between the blade and the apple. There it remained firmly wedged until I lifted the knife. No wonder I'm gray.

For all his cleverness, Chip could be fooled at times by deceptive surfaces. Two or three times, he landed on a sheet of paper I was examining only to be humiliated by it instantly collapsing beneath him. On another memorable occasion when I was doing the laundry, he jumped down confidently onto the thin film of suds in the machine only to find himself suddenly out of his depth, thrashing wildly. Mercifully, I was on the spot, having turned my back for only a moment.

Chip's unending activity could also be exasperating. A horrendous crash in the kitchen one afternoon revealed shattered glass strewn over a huge bowl of chopped mixed vegetables, freshly steamed for winter storage in the freezer. The carefully-saved stock destined for soup also had to be discarded while the smashed glass panel on the stove needed to be covered permanently with strong tape for safety's sake.

At times like these, one longs to be able to swallow several capsules of instant patience with a glass of water—or something stronger.

Then one morning in late August Chip began to act extremely restless, zipping from window to window, 'chucking' loudly as he watched the outside grackles. I had no doubt that he longed to be with them.

I pondered his situation: he was now able to shell and eat oats, having often watched adult grackles through the one-way-glass feeder; to a hearty, full-grown grackle, the already small house might become too small; he still was bothered with a sneezy cough despite treatment but otherwise radiated health and energy; however, his trust in humans was still intact—and this last was an issue that really worried me. To confine him against his will, though, was unthinkable. I had to hope that he'd learn distrust by associating and migrating with other grackles.

I carried him outside.

For the next few weeks, I watched Chip enjoying the natural world, searching for insects up in the trees and down on the ground, and I marvelled at the unusual crevices wherein his probing bill met with success. He was easily distinguished at a distance since his new adult tail was still lengthening and was only two inches long. Nearly all his juvenile plumage had been replaced by adult feathering and his head now shone with teal iridescence. By the following spring, his dark eyes would probably be golden yellow.

Ten days earlier, I'd built him a wall-mounted feeder in the studio and now I saw him frequenting the outdoor feeders with the ease of familiarity. However, flock after flock of wild grackles departed for the South without him. Occasionally, I saw him in the company of stragglers but sooner or later, they moved on.

Still, Chip stayed.

I began once more to wonder if he had imprinted upon humans before I took him in—and, if he had, whether he'd ever truly become a wild grackle. I felt certain, too, that Chip felt torn between the lure of the natural world with his own kind and the pull of indoor life with me. I was feeling very divided myself, but strove to keep his best interests as my guide.

Year by year, the marvel of migration has deepened within me. Many birds don't survive it, for the hazards are innumerable, and some fail to make a proper start.

Late one fall, years earlier, I noticed a juvenile grackle coming to the feeder. He clearly wasn't a strong healthy bird so I kept a close watch on him and put out plenty of seed. Early in December, the temperature plunged very low overnight and frosty arabesques danced across the windows. The snow squealed under my boots as I stepped outside to feed the birds.

As I approached with a container of seeds, I spotted the grackle huddled in the corner of the feeder. When he saw me, he turned his head away and cringed against the sides, lacking the strength to zoom past me to safety. I knew I had to grab him successfully on the first try. Otherwise, weakened as he was, he would lead me a merry chase through the drifts and snow-laden bushes. Taking a deep breath, I dropped the seeds and charged suddenly, seizing the startled bird. Cradling him as gently as possible, I galloped into the house and released him inside the studio. Next, I scattered seeds across the floor and withdrew behind the wire mesh door to watch surreptitiously. Within a short while, the warmth had quickened his energies and he was eating hungrily.

'Chuck' the grackle was in for the winter.

I called him Chuck as I had with an earlier grackle because of the distinctive 'chuck' call that grackles emit. He was an excellent guest and within days was eating and bathing calmly only a few feet from me as I painted. Even flying chips of wood on my vigorous carving days failed to disturb him but he never landed on me and I made no advances. I just wanted him to live as he wished and be free in the spring.

I fed him a varied diet of wild birdseed and human food, and wormed him after he passed an internal parasite. It was this last, I suspected, that had caused the decline in his condition which in turn had prevented his migration.

When the grackles returned in the spring, I released a sleek, golden-eyed Chuck who clearly lacked the striking iridescent head of the males.

Chuck was destined to lay eggs!

MEANWHILE, each day Chip would swoop down out of the trees and land on me with every indication that an offering of mealworms would be welcomed. I'd resist the temptation to comply, preferring him to find wild food instead, and would show him moths resting on the wall near the outside light, or would turn over the occasional rock so he could snap up sowbugs and centipedes. His reflexes seemed to quicken more each day, and he seemed ever more suspicious and alert for any hint of danger—which was very reassuring. Friends arriving with a gift of corn borers and cabbage worms were delighted to watch Chip descend from the trees to my hand, snatch a writhing beakful and carry his booty to the roof—in case the rest of us should be tempted to partake!

These days I was wheeling loads of firewood up the path from the pasture each morning and stacking them inside the woodshed. As usual, I was 'helped' by Bubble and Squeak who were carefully de-bugging each load. Chip rapidly caught on, even climbing into the wheelbarrow to snare his prey or riding into the woodshed on top of an armload, anxious to miss nothing. Very soon, all three birds were accompanying me back and forth from the woodpile and vying with one another for the scuttling inhabitants.

One morning as I loaded the barrow and Chip searched the

dwindling woodpile for bugs, I wondered uneasily what he'd do if a hawk suddenly materialized when I wasn't on the spot. The firewood was dumped in the open field and Chip's apprehension always became more pronounced whenever we left the shelter of the trees surrounding the house and woodsheds. Would he try to hide among the chunks of wood? Or would he attempt to fly as far as the bushes nearby? Surely this last would be chancey.

At that precise moment in my meditations, a bluejay screamed a warning and I had my answer.

In a flash, Chip had shot into a deep crevice in the woodpile and completely disappeared from view. When the jays sounded the 'all clear,' Chip's glossy head cautiously emerged unscathed.

I was very impressed.

Flit, meanwhile, was learning to nourish himself in ways wholly at variance to his swallow heritage. I taped a small, shallow dish to his branches and loaded it with mealworms. Swallows eat during flight so I felt that he would learn to eat more readily if the dish were at 'tree-top' level rather than down on a table. With his extremely short legs and slight grip, he was unable to reach down into a deeper dish without tumbling in. Even to move along the edge of the dish, he raised his wings upright and vibrated them to assist his sideways pattering locomotion, since the legs of swallows aren't designed to stride or hop. Although a shallow dish therefore was necessary, a certain depth was also needed to restrain the mealworms and eventually I found the ideal container. The mealies, too, were large, awkward fare for Flit's tiny mouth, unlike light flying insects, but he'd grab them by their middles and manoeuvre them in manfully. He ate a surprising quantity at each meal for such a small bird.

I also provided him with a similar dish for water, another anti-instinctual set-up, since swallows drink on the wing, cleaving the surface of a pond with wide-open beaks. This, too, was difficult for Flit and he'd intuitively open his beak to its fullest extent and bob it into the water, gulping awkwardly. I often had to ripple the water as well, to trigger him.

Bathing presented unusual considerations since, whenever I set up a wide, shallow dish of water and tickled the surface invitingly, Flit, rather than stepping in and beating his wings as I expected, 'belly-flopped' and immediately soared around the room shedding a fine spray. I'd set him before the water a second and even a third time with exactly the same results until he was satisfied. It was obvious that swallows also bathe in flight but occasionally Flit lingered in the water and beat his wings in the more common manner, once again compromising for my inadequate substitutions.

In time I was able to relocate Flit's food and water dishes on a special shelf built beside his branches since I'd found it difficult to clean the dishes properly when they were taped in place.

As he gradually conquered each of these challenges, I couldn't fail to be impressed by tiny Flit's intrepid adaptability.

THE LOCAL raccoon population had again exploded and often I was awakened at night as they romped up and down the roof just over my head, or twanged their way across the weasel screening on the porch. Feeders were damaged, excrement lay everywhere underfoot and the outside waterdish left so disgustingly despoiled each morning that I decided grimly to move the rascals elsewhere. With such numbers I worried, too, about any possible threat to the roosters.

Accordingly, I set my own trap as well as a borrowed one, trapping over a dozen in all. Then I bravely hoisted the snarling cages into the wheelbarrow, trundled them to the van and released them many miles away in a chickenless area. Though accumulated dirt and droppings were thoroughly swept out of the van after each run, I still had a horror of any external parasites lingering behind. When I looked at the thickness of raccoon fur, I couldn't help but feel that each creature was easily capable of accomodating tarantulas and no one would be the wiser. I also left the van windows down all day.

Raccoons reek.

As I returned one morning with my emptied cages, Chip bounced down onto my shoulder and I sank down onto a bench for a visit. Three busy weeks had passed since I'd carried him outside and although his sneezy cough had persisted, he looked gorgeous—big, glossy and iridescent, his tail lengthening nicely. The heavy, humid atmosphere muffled all the usual sounds, creating one of those noticeably silent days that must have been the norm in the morning of the world. Suddenly, my contentment was shattered. I heard ominous sounds from inside Chip—a rattley rumble with every breath that indicated pulmonary problems. The nights now were damp and very chilly and I had strong doubts as to whether Chip was considering migrating. I also doubted that he could with an internal infection so I decided to bring him inside for the winter and treat him once more with tetracycline.

Chip enjoyed being indoors as much as outdoors but tiny Flit bristled with indignation at this invasion of (now) his territory. He fluttered belligerently in front of big burly Chip till Chip finally snapped at him as at an annoying mosquito. If he caught Flit, he just tweaked him enough to get his point across and thankfully indicated no aggressive intentions. Oftimes, he chased Flit teasingly, perhaps even threatening him off a lampshade but showed no desire really to hurt him. In fact, Chip taught Flit by example many new landing sites so that often I saw Flit sitting defiantly in a new locale—a spot Chip had vacated moments earlier.

Chip showed jealousy, too, whenever Flit sat under my chin singing his enchanting profusion of chirps and warbles and squeaks. Bristling, Chip would thump onto my shoulder and the glare in his eyes would melt away only if I welcomed him warmly and divided my attentions between them.

However, with a crafty grackle exploring every crevice in the house, I was unable to leave mealworms openly in Flit's dish. I resorted to providing them as soon as I saw Flit fly to his shelf looking for food, or kept a hidden supply near me if I were busy in another part of the house. Then I offered them on a regular basis. When I left the house for an extended length of time, I divided the premises with a sheet—Chip on one side and Flit on the other—so that I could leave food out for Flit in his usual place.

After all Flit's intensive learning and cooperative compromising, I was forced finally to introduce consistent confusion.

Meanwhile, I began treating Chip with tetracycline and the sounds in his lungs gradually diminished while the familiar sneezy cough persisted. He slept at night with his beak pointed up instead of tucked under his wing in order to keep his breathing passages clear, and the medication was unable to change this. Not for months was he able to sleep normally, and even then suffered periodic relapses.

Initially, I was successful in disguising the medicine in little food pellets but Chip was too foxy for that method to last long. I was soon driven to holding him physically, which he disliked, and trickling the fluid down his throat. Of course, this soon developed into a 'catch me if you can' game with Chip. His argument, that he loathed the taste, was severely undermined each time when he voluntarily drank up stray drops on the hand that was holding him—but at least we had another new game.

Professional advice concluded that Chip had a chronic virus and confirmed my own suspicions that he had developed it in his early days while caged. He wasn't kept as warm as necessary for a youngster, his immune system had been damaged and the confinement had induced stress. The virus would be a lifelong handicap, rather like emphyzema in humans, undoubtedly cancelling any potential for migration, and would be worse at stressful times when he would require, again, tetracycline. Hopefully, the other birds, being healthy adults, wouldn't contract the virus.

Chip's high spirits and bounding energies remained undisturbed by the virus and he constantly evolved new ways of entertaining himself. In the tiny bathroom, he instigated his bizarre 'helicopter act.' Whenever I was 'using the facilities,' he'd suddenly hurl himself up to the shower rod, down to my head, up to the shelf, over to the shower rod, back to the towel hook, down to my head and so on—over and over, up and down, back and forth and all at top speed. It was great fun for both of us.

One evening, as I sat with the roosters slumbering in my lap and Chip rooting through my pockets for his hidden toys, I slipped a cassette of nature sounds into my portable player. At once, the headphones resounded with trilling frogs, barking foxes and bird calls. Chip was utterly fascinated. A flock of crows sent him scuttling under the chair and calling grackles had him prying up the earphones and answering them. The roosters, too, were intrigued and mingled their territorial crowing with the cacophony in my ears.

Another day, having discovered a few small cabbages and heads of celery amongst the bounty of slugs in my garden, I decided to make a winter's supply of soup—and Chip 'helped.' Throughout the morning, I washed and chopped veggies, mounding them up in the big pot, with the onions tossed in at the last. Then I turned on the heat and began gathering discarded leaves and trimmings, as well as a few stray slugs for the chickens. Flit had sat on top of the spice cabinet, his beady eyes brightly watching the whole process and had been regaled frequently with juicy cabbage worms. Chip, revelling in the confusion, had so excited himself bobbing after stray bits of flotsam in the bowl of muddy wash-water that he'd finally leaped in for an exhilarating bath, leaving brown streams running down the walls and puddles all over the counter.

I began mopping around the sink and when the counter was finally cleared, I crouched on the floor, wiping it clean. As I worked, I suddenly found myself being bombarded with onions and stood up, curious.

Chip was *inside* the soup pot as it heated, 'anting' frenziedly with peeled onions, the more slippery pieces squirting out of his mouth, rebounding off the fridge and walls and skidding across the floor. Flit fluttered erratically above the pot, chittering in annoyance and dodging the flying onions. A piece of floating onion circled languidly in my mug of fresh coffee.

Once again, I felt I was in for an interesting winter.

LATER THAT EVENING, after the soup had attained a savoury peak—without the questionable seasonings of grackle toes and swallow droppings—and was cooling on the counter, the birds and I sat companionably in the living room. Beyond the windows, an icy green afterglow darkened the surrounding trees. As usual, Bubble and Squeak slumbered contentedly across me, their beautiful plumage flowing in shimmering waves, like a waterfall, over my quickly numbing legs. Flit cozied down on my finger, chattering softly, his light touch almost imperceptible. Chip slid about on my head playing with a small rubbery dinosaur, dropping it from time to time on Squeak's back and narrowly missing Flit (with unconvincing innocence). My part in this 'game' consisted of disturbing Squeak as often as possible by rooting around under his recumbent, protesting form, searching for and returning the dinosaur. In the darkened studio, Molly and Desmond dozed peacefully.

I reflected on how fortunate I was to be living in such a continual whirl of avian entertainment, watching individual personalites unfold in unpredictable ways, gaining invaluable insights for my work and my life. I certainly ran little risk of being bored, although during our more chaotic times, I pondered the possibility almost wistfully.

When I contemplated my own death, as one does at times, I remembered the dying gull I'd held in my arms. How could one infuse fear into such an uplifting experience?

In the tranquillity of the evening, I remembered feeding nestlings, teaching them those small elements of survival that were within my limited human capabilities, watching with a full heart as they finally soared up into the trees on their own. I carried the hope that my little bit of help, combined with the mysterious workings of their ancestral memories, would culminate in thousands of miles of successful migrating. Equating migrations around me with my inner migration, that arduous transformative process towards the light, towards spring and renewal, makes my own struggle worthwhile and gives meaning to my spiritual journey.

I thought of Bubble and Squeak, and Chip too, greeting each morning as though this were the morning for which they had been waiting. I recalled Rubble, that irrepressible duck, her freshness and vitality, her gift for living in the present which is the norm for all birds yet a pinnacle for human spiritual adepts. We, who are continually oscillating between remembering and forgetting, between anticipating and regretting, would be wise to emulate our avian 'elders' in their capacity to live fully in the present moment and welcome each dawn as if it were the first.

I can't imagine ever fully developing those avian qualities of which I am becoming more aware daily. But surely even partially fulfilling such an aspiration would benefit ourselves and our fellow creatures. Although I am a long way from such an inner awakening, by honouring each present moment, when I remember, is to make a beginning.

And the birds will show me the way.

The Quest, *linoprint.*